More Praise for *The Power of Pictures*

"Through powerful examples of students' work, thoughtful explanations, and clear, simple instructions, Beth guides us into a revolutionary way of teaching writing that ensures all children are successful. Having used this art-based approach to writing for the last nine years, I can attest to its ability to empower all learners!"
—Paula Kilts, teacher, grade 2, Northeast Elementary School, Ithaca, New York

"Olshansky has created a model based on how kids learn, a model that draws on the best tool—our ability to think in pictures. Don't let this one pass you by; it is sure to bring positive results for all learners, but especially those who need it the most."
—Marcia McCaffrey, arts education consultant, Bureau of Accountability, New Hampshire Department of Education

"During our ten years of implementing the Artists/Writers Workshop, teachers consistently reported how students who had difficulty expressing themselves, and completing writing assignments, became creative and engaged writers using this arts-based approach. I strongly recommend this book to district administrators, principals, and teachers."
—Charles Parchment, Ph.D., (retired) director of language development, Franklin-McKinley School District, San Jose, California

"All teachers and parents should read *The Power of Pictures* in order to fully understand how students can use their natural visual abilities to improve their literacy skills. Beth Olshansky's extensive and impressive research provides a very convincing rationale for promoting a strong visual and verbal partnership in the curricula of our schools."
—Janet L. Olson, Ed.D., author of *Envisioning Writing* and professor emeritus, Department of Visual Arts, Boston University

"Picturing Writing has been a godsend process for our self-contained ELL classroom. It gives *all* our refugee and immigrant students a voice despite their diverse backgrounds. We have witnessed tremendous growth in all aspects of language development!"
—Kristen Beakey and Donna Papanikolau, ELL classroom teachers, grades 3-5, Webster Elementary School, Manchester, New Hampshire

"Beth Olshansky's book and DVD set is extremely valuable for teachers and teacher preparation programs. Practical and theoretically grounded, this is an excellent introduction to a broader view of literacy and a lasting resource for teachers."
—J. David Betts, assistant professor, language, reading, and culture, University of Arizona

"The Picturing Writing program is arts integration at its best—a perfect combination of literacy and the arts—where drawing and painting become vehicles for learning to write."
—Ray Doughty, former project director, South Carolina
Arts in Basic Curriculum (ABC) Project

"Last year I tried this approach with my class of high school special education students. This diverse group all experienced an enormous sense of pride and self-worth as they artfully crafted their own spectacular picture books. In the process, the students made tremendous improvements in their reading and writing skills, which also carried over into their test scores!"
—Cindy Helmbreck, Academic Support Reading/English,
Salem High School, Salem, Massachusetts

"I've had great success using these methods with English Language Learners and other at-risk students. Engaging *all* learners, this visual approach promotes oral language skills and writing that flow directly from the pictures students have painted with care and pride. *The Power of Pictures* will be required reading in my university literacy courses!"
—Donna L. Garcia, Ph.D., instructor, language, literacy, and sociocultural studies,
College of Education, University of New Mexico

"While others talk about the need to provide diversely talented, struggling students an alternative to traditional methods when learning reading and writing, Beth Olshansky has built them a lifeboat. *The Power of Pictures* should be all anyone needs to break away once and for all from conventional 'verbocentric' teaching practices."
—Emily Pike, enrichment specialist, Bedwell Elementary School, Bernardsville, New Jersey

"If you wrestle with the current high-stakes testing climate and find it an anathema to inspired learning, this single book is a "must read!" I have experienced few such literacy models that children, pre-adolescents, and adolescents of all learning styles and abilities love and that demonstrate improved reading and writing."
—Janet Curcio Wilson, dean of special education, Newport Middle School,
Newport, New Hampshire

"This solid literacy framework is infused with an innovative art-based alternative that taps into the source of all good writing—making pictures inside and outside your head. Beth Olshansky has made a significant contribution to expanding our view of literacy and what effective literacy instruction should be."
—Claudia E. Cornett, Ph.D., professor emerita, Wittenberg University,
and author of *Creating Meaning Through Literature and the Arts*

"Every elementary student deserves to experience an artist's pathway to their writing. Beth Olshansky has spent twenty years sharing her 'artist to author' process in workshops throughout the U.S. and beyond. This book, at last, gives everyone access to her innovative approach."
—Chris Kapololu, librarian/teacher, Keaukaha Elementary School, Hilo, Hawaii

"Rich with compelling portraits of learners, beautiful examples of student work, and practical guidance for implementation, this book is not only highly readable but also contains convincing evidence of student achievement."
—Tracie Costantino, Ph.D., assistant professor of art education, University of Georgia

"Each time I use Beth's Picturing Writing or Image-Making process with a new group of pupils, I am struck anew by the deep level of engagement and sustained motivation in my at-risk Title I children—they are so proud of their work! Beth's ability to communicate the value of visual and kinesthetic activities in our classrooms has transformed my work with at-risk students."
—Katherine Lovering Shanks, Title I project manager, Monadnock Regional School District, Swanzey, New Hampshire

"Relevant for all teachers and administrators, Beth Olshansky's Artists/Writers Workshop is a place where learners of all styles and languages are empowered by the artist's brush and the writer's pen to weave stories of exceptional quality."
—Jasmin A. Niedo, School of Education, Northern Marianas College, Saipan

"Artists/Writers Workshop gives students the tools they need to create beautiful pictures and extraordinary writing. The DVD brings Artists/Writers Workshop to life! This book is a must for teachers."
—Patricia Semrick, teacher of grades 1, 2, 6, 7, and 8, Bullard TALENT K-8, Fresno, California

"I have never in my thirty years seen first graders write like this or be so attuned to literature. This approach works for my low readers and writers; it challenges my top students; and it supports those in the middle."
—Merrilee Thissell, former assistant principal and first grade teacher, Hallsville Elementary School, Manchester, New Hampshire

"Beth Olshansky generously shares a teaching approach perfected through years of successful classroom practice, and inspired by the conviction that visual art and writing are 'equal, parallel, and complementary languages.' The children's resulting work testifies to the power of the carefully scaffolded learning process she recommends."
    —Christine Marmé Thompson, professor of art education, Pennsylvania State University

"Olshansky's well-documented research clearly shows that literacy—even in the lowest of achievers—can blossom when the classroom teacher also employs the parallel language of visual expression. The results are stunning, artful, and imaginative—a clear testament to a method that yields dramatic improvement and empowers young learners!"
    —Sally Gradle, Ed.D. art education, Southern Illinois University, Carbondale

"Beth's book and DVD will speak to the hearts of teachers who want more children to succeed as writers and learners. It describes Artists/Writers Workshop and delivers deep insight into the wondrous potential of learning through the parallel and equal languages of pictures and words."
    —Beth Berghoff, associate professor of language education, Indiana University

"Beth Olshansky's Picturing Writing and Image-Making descriptions are a breath of fresh air for improvement of language arts. Exploration of these techniques at George Mason University with struggling adolescent readers has been equally as effective as those reported in this well-written, step-by-step approach that honors learners with alternative learning styles. I highly recommend this book for teachers across grade levels."
    —Barbara K. Given, Ph.D. co-director, Adolescent and Adult Learning Research Center, Krasnow Institute for Advanced Study, George Mason University

"*The Power of Pictures* book/DVD provides a unique contribution to classroom teachers and other professionals who value the visual arts but are unsure of why or how art can contribute to literacy in the elementary classroom. Olshansky writes with authority, providing solid theory and research to support her exciting practical suggestions."
    —Barbara Kiefer, Charlotte S. Huck Professor of Children's Literature, Ohio State University.

"Beth Olshansky's system for integrating art and literacy development creates in students young and old a zest for learning. It creates confident and competent students and improves the quality of their work to a remarkable degree. Extraordinary!"
    —Mary Jo Morris, Ph.D., learning disabilities consultant, Humber College, Toronto, Ontario.

Jossey-Bass
Teacher

Jossey-Bass Teacher provides educators with practical knowledge and tools to create a positive and lifelong impact on student learning. We offer classroom-tested and research-based teaching resources for a variety of grade levels and subject areas. Whether you are an aspiring, new, or veteran teacher, we want to help you make every teaching day your best.

From ready-to-use classroom activities to the latest teaching framework, our value-packed books provide insightful, practical, and comprehensive materials on the topics that matter most to K–12 teachers. We hope to become your trusted source for the best ideas from the most experienced and respected experts in the field.

The Power of Pictures

Creating Pathways to Literacy Through Art, Grades K–6

Beth Olshansky

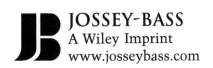

JOSSEY-BASS
A Wiley Imprint
www.josseybass.com

Published by Jossey-Bass
A Wiley Imprint
989 Market Street, San Francisco, CA 94103-1741—www.josseybass.com

Library of Congress Cataloging-in-Publication Data

Olshansky, Beth, 1950–
    The power of pictures : creating pathways to literacy through art, grades K–6 / Beth Olshansky.
       p.   cm.
   Includes bibliographical references and index.
      ISBN 978-0-7879-9667-3
       1. Visual learning—United States.   2. Art in education—United States.   3. Language arts (Elementary)—United States.   I. Title.
   LB1067.5.O47   2008
   372.5—dc22
                                                                                    2008003849

Printed in the United States of America
FIRST EDITION
PB Printing   10 9 8 7 6 5 4 3 2 1

Contents

Preface

Pictures provide a universal language. They speak equally to native speakers of English, to those learning English as a second language, and to those who simply struggle with words in any language. They have deep roots in our history, both as individuals and as a species. Indeed, pictures are our first written language, whether we consider human evolution or the stages of development imprinted in our individual DNA. As our first written language, pictures offer a language we all intuitively understand.

Over the last two decades, I have had the opportunity to work with thousands of students and teachers across diverse regions and within various educational settings—from a one-room schoolhouse in northern New England to several large urban schools in California, from remote schoolhouses in landlocked villages on the Alaskan tundra (where students must learn to write in Yup'ik) to Hawaiian immersion schools on the shores of the Big Island to village schools on the islands of Saipan, American Samoa, and Puerto Rico. As my students, fellow teachers, and I worked together to explore the parallel and complementary languages of pictures and words, the opportunity to observe a wide range of learners—of varying ages and abilities, from diverse cultures and speaking diverse languages, and clearly with diverse learning styles—has allowed me to dig deeper into the many ways in which creating pictures before writing can support the literacy learning—learning of reading as well as writing—of all learners.

Understanding Parallel Languages

Pictures truly are a language in their own right, not simply a decorative adjunct to so-called true—verbal—language. As a visual language, which runs parallel to our own verbal language, it is possible to teach the very same literary elements through the language of pictures as through the language of words. Take the element of *setting,* for example: just as you can analyze how the first paragraphs of text establish a sense of setting and mood at the beginning of a story, you can also analyze the "setting picture" in a quality picture book, noting how it establishes a sense of setting and mood through the use of visual elements. Through literature studies of both pictures and words, students of all ages come to understand not only the literary parallels but also how the two languages complement each other and work together to more fully express what each alone cannot entirely convey.

By placing art and the study of quality picture books at the center of literacy learning, the process I describe moves beyond using art merely as a carrot to entice reluctant writers or as a reward for completing writing. It moves beyond using art as a springboard for writing (as when we tell students, "Make a picture and write about it"). Instead, it provides concrete visual, tactual, and kinesthetic tools for learners at each and every stage of the writing process. As students gain access to multiple modes of thinking, they enter the reading/writing process from a position of personal strength and enthusiasm supported—rather than hindered—by their individual learning style.

The art-based literacy model described in this book is democratic and inclusive. It fosters engaged learning communities by drawing on the strengths of all classroom members. It provides daily opportunities for all students to be honored for the strengths they possess rather than penalized for the ones they don't. It presents systematic daily literacy instruction that employs multiple modes of thinking at every stage of the writing process and thus ensures the enthusiastic participation and engagement of all learners. It offers a carefully crafted, lively alternative pathway into literacy learning for those who struggle with the language of words. For those students who are comfortable users of words, it provides opportunities to stretch and grow in new directions while strengthening their facility with words even further. As for teachers, it provides new tools for fostering a genuine learning community that reaches every member of the classroom—and results in solid literacy gains that are reflected in students' standardized test scores in both writing and reading.

Especially today, with educators and administrators living in the shadow of No Child Left Behind, it is more clear than ever before that we need to move beyond our verbocentric approach to teaching reading and writing, an approach that clearly does not work for all students. We need to offer our students an alternative.

I write this book to offer one such alternative. Drawing from nearly two decades of work in the trenches developing, field-testing, and refining an innovative art-based approach to literacy learning, in this book and companion DVD I share simple, concrete methods that are both uncommon and uncommonly effective, particularly for those who "learn differently." I also present research as well as standardized test score data that documents the dramatic impact this approach can have on the reading and writing skills of low-performing students. As an advocate for creating an educational system that is inclusive and democratic in nature, I invite educators to rethink our most basic assumptions about what comprises effective literacy practice and instruction.

Outline of the Book

This book is divided into two sections. Part One lays down the foundation for an art-based approach to literacy learning. Chapter One introduces the use of art to drive rather than simply adorn the writing process—why it works, and what it can help us accomplish. In Chapter Two, I discuss the theoretical basis for this approach.

Part Two discusses the art-based literacy model I have developed, outlining what has proven to be one very effective way of bringing art-based literacy instruction into the classroom. Although this approach concentrates on the interaction between art and writing, its impact on reading is immediate, apparent, and telling. I devote Chapter Three to that topic. Chapters Four through Six address the use of art and exactly how it can be utilized to enhance thinking, writing, and revision. In Chapter Seven, I discuss the preparation and assessment of lessons. In Chapter Eight, I open the door to developing visual literacy by discussing how two favorite picture book illustrators have used the language of pictures to make meaning. Chapters Eight and Nine, both offer mini-lessons ready for use in the classroom. Chapter Ten provides two compelling stories of what can happen when we rethink the way we teach.

One of the most promising aspects of this dynamic approach to literacy learning is that it is not an add-on but rather a way of presenting mandated curriculum so as to captivate your students and enhance their learning. Appendix A summarizes the research that has been conducted thus far to measure the effects of this approach. It also offers reading and writing standardized test score data comparing the results of students participating in art-based literacy practices to those in traditional classrooms. Appendix B presents an explanation of several instructional tools that enhance the workshop process and make it run smoothly.

The companion DVD included with this book offers a peek into the classroom. It provides a comprehensive overview of the workshop model, live classroom demonstrations, and explicit visual instruction. As a visual learner given the task of conveying a visual process through words, I welcome the opportunity to show you as well as tell you about the work.

Who Is This Book For?

This book is written primarily for classroom teachers of grades 1–6, though this art-based approach to literacy learning has been used successfully with kindergarteners as well as middle school and high school students. This approach will also be of interest to art and reading specialists, Title I and special education teachers, teachers of gifted and talented students, as well as teachers of English language learners. Parents and administrators will find the ideas presented within this book worthy of serious consideration as they search for methods for turning around some of our schools' toughest educational challenges.

Teachers considering trying this approach in their classrooms need not feel apprehensive because of a lack of background or ease with art; this art-and-literature-based approach to writing assumes no prior art knowledge. It is designed as a progression of experiences that begins very simply and builds on acquired skill so that even those (teachers and students) with no art background can gain comfort and ease with this approach. The introductory sample lessons have been "crash-tested" with the youngest of artists and the most reluctant of teachers.

For those who feel apprehensive about shifting to a whole new way of thinking about teaching writing—indeed, about literacy learning!—let me assure you that a solid literacy model is embedded within this innovative art-based alternative framework. There is nothing "fluffy" about this approach. Rather, every literature study, every modeling session, every art and writing experience, and every group share and discussion is designed around specific literacy and literary goals. Systematic daily infusions of art-and-literature-based writing mini-lessons, delivered through the dual language of pictures and words, maintain a steady stream of instruction while at the same time speaking the language of the students who need that instruction the most.

Don't be surprised if this seemingly indirect pathway into literacy learning helps your students find new and stronger voices and fosters a new excitement about reading and writing in your classroom. Don't be surprised if parents come to you in disbelief because their child has produced such impressive art and writing. And don't be surprised to hear your struggling readers and writers making comments like David's "I didn't know I could do that good!" I invite you to join me in recognizing the power of pictures to transform the literacy learning—and the lives—of your students.

January 2008

Beth Olshansky
Durham, New Hampshire

Acknowledgments

One day in May 1990, I stopped by Creative Classrooms in Raymond, New Hampshire, looking for recycled materials to use in the creative dance classes I was teaching. I began talking with Moon Morgan, their office manager. One thing led to another and before I knew it, I was telling him about an idea I had had six years earlier to integrate art into the writing process. Moon expressed interest in this notion and offered to write a grant proposal to submit to the New Hampshire State Council on the Arts, due the next week! Never having considered this possibility before, I told him I would think about it overnight. I did, and in the morning I accepted his offer. This very first grant proposal, submitted with the blessings of Fritz Bell, founder and director of Creative Classrooms, launched my explorations in art and writing in September of 1990. To Fritz, Moon, and Creative Classrooms, I am forever indebted.

Over the past eighteen years, I have been blessed with the opportunity to work alongside many dedicated and gifted teachers. Each, in some way, has contributed to the overall development of this body of work, and for this I am grateful. In the very beginning, Principal Jean Robbins welcomed me into her school and Barbara Rynerson into her classroom. Barbara became my first mentor as I explored the collage process as a tool for supporting the literacy learning of her first- and second-grade students. She was also adventurous enough to agree to have videographers come into her classroom to capture the Image-Making collage process firsthand.

Ann Jule, friend, colleague, and fellow right-brain thinker, shared her enthusiasm and expertise early on, offering fascinating insights into the inner workings of the brains of young artists and writers.

Penny Clare and Gail Gagnon joined my research efforts early in the process, welcoming me into their classrooms and then spending the next decade refining the work. When I first received federal funding for national dissemination in 1993 through the National Diffusion Network, Penny and Gail, along with Tess Hall, became my first certified trainers, traveling to faraway places to share their expertise before I was ready to get on an airplane. When I was finally willing to fly, Chris Kapololu of Hawaii became an immediate colleague. Chris was never shy about offering suggestions—for which I remain grateful. I want to thank all the teachers in Saipan, American Samoa, Puerto Rico, Alaska, and Hawaii who embraced my ideas about art-based literacy on their islands (even those villages in Alaska were landlocked and islands unto themselves) and offered many opportunities to explore art and writing within the context of their rich cultural heritages. These were experiences of a lifetime, ones I never dreamed of having.

Back home, Sue Rafferty called me up one day looking for glue sticks and ended up luring me into her classroom to explore art-based literacy more deeply. I spent two years in Sue's classroom developing Picturing Writing and refining the Image-Making process. Sue's deep appreciation for each of her students, her passion for creating strong writers, and her eagerness to share her observations offered me a particularly rich learning environment. We spent hours musing over her students' work as we watched her first graders become artists and writers extraordinaire. It was Sue who observed one day that all it takes is a sneeze to revise a student's collage story (yet to be glued). Margo Carrier also took me under her wing, showing me new heights of organization both in her classroom and within the work itself. Susan O'Byrne nearly dropped out of our second research study for fear she couldn't make the commitment and then, with a little encouragement, dove in headfirst and hasn't come up for air ever since. Susan has become a master teacher and trainer, having used Image-Making and Picturing Writing in her classroom now going on 15 years. Carol LaChance also joined our research efforts in 1997 and continues to integrate the process into the curriculum in her gifted-and-talented classes at a variety of grade levels. Title I Chair Kathy Shanks has also been a longtime friend and colleague, sharing her expertise and enthusiasm in a way that is absolutely contagious. Art specialists Sue Bonnin Nylander, Sally Bent, Sharon Santillo, and Colleen Schmidt pioneered the work in their art rooms in four different schools in three different states, decorating their hallways with students' art and writing and capturing the interest of their teachers and administrators. Each has served as a catalyst for school-wide (or greater) adoptions.

I am grateful to Dr. Sue O'Connor for providing me with an opportunity of a lifetime when she wrote, received, and administered a three-year Comprehensive School Reform Demonstration grant to integrate Picturing Writing and Image-Making into her school's language arts, science, and art curriculum. This school-wide adoption, now in its eighth year, has provided a wealth of experiences with an entire staff and the opportunity to follow students' standardized test score data in reading and writing over time. I am grateful to the entire staff at Main Street School for contributing their expertise to the development of several integrated curriculum units. Joyce Bosch and Linda Ball also agreed to share their expertise and allow their classrooms to become sites for filming my first DVD (no small matter).

Reading specialist Patty Giguere first brought Picturing Writing and Image-Making to Manchester, NH (a city that serves as a National Refugee Relocation Center), where she experienced its power with students from all over the world. Her ongoing enthusiasm and hard work ultimately resulted in Manchester being awarded an Arts in Education Model Development and Dissemination (AEMDD) grant to conduct a large research study which is now underway in the district. I am grateful to the 50-plus teachers I am currently working with in Manchester, their principals, reading specialists, and support staff for providing a wonderfully rich environment for further inquiry. Hallsville first-grade teacher, assistant principal, and Picturing Writing enthusiast Merrilee Thissell recently retired only to become the AEMDD district coordinator in Manchester. I am grateful to Merrilee for helping oversee the project as well as sharing her enthusiasm and expertise with her colleagues. Special thanks to Krystie Fleming and Jamie Bressler for allowing me to film in their classrooms. Jamie's third-grade students appear in the companion DVD and Krystie's first graders will appear in a DVD I have yet to produce. Thank you to all their students for being such good teachers of the work. I also offer my sincere appreciation to Kristen Beakey, Donna Papanikolau, Vanessa Rashid, and Katherine Frink for welcoming me into their ELL classrooms to work with students from all over the world. What a wonderful experience!

I want to thank Dr. Susan Frankel for contributing her expertise in the area of research design to the project. Susan has worked with me since the beginning, designing our first, second, and now third research studies. Though we struggled in the beginning to find a common language, we have grown to respect and appreciate each other's left-brain/right-brain ways of thinking. I have come to realize that, like the pictures and words, you need both to tell the whole story.

I also want to thank my team of east-coast and west-coast certified trainers—on the east coast, Gail Gagnon, Susan O'Byrne, Penny Clare, Kathy Shanks, Carol LaChance, Sharon Santillo, Gerry Vagos, Paula Kilts, and Merrilee Thissell; and on the west coast, Sue Bonnin Nylander, Pat Semrick, Amanda Urrutia-Rayburn, Jan Morita, Sally Bent, Carolyn Franks, and Donna Garcia—for sharing their expertise. I would like to express my appreciation to Marcia McCaffrey, visual arts consultant for the State of New Hampshire, Margaret Kelley and Suzanne McDonald, for listening and offering their perspectives from time to time. My partner Don Brautigam has offered his technical assistance (not my area of expertise) ever since I began this work in the schools in 1990. I am grateful for his unending patience.

There also have been literally hundreds of teachers who have invited me into their classrooms or who have attended a teacher workshop over the years who have impressed me with their dedication, hard work, and eagerness to explore this visual/verbal arena. I thank them (and their principals) for helping to further this body of work. My life's work has been enriched because of you.

I am grateful for the generous support I have received over the years from the New Hampshire State Council on the Arts, the Christos Papoutsy Foundation, the Walker Fund, the Frances R. Dewing Foundation, the Fuller Foundation, the Greater Piscataqua Community Foundation, the Greater Portsmouth Educational Partnership Council, the DuPont Foundation, the Ella Lyman Cabot Trust, and the U.S. Department of Education's National Diffusion Network, Comprehensive School Reform Demonstration program and Arts in Education Model Development and Dissemination program. There have been many other foundations and organizations that have directly supported school projects over the years. I express my thanks to them as well.

If you have ever called my office, you have spoken with Liz Arcieri. Liz has managed my office at the Center for the Advancement of Art-Based Literacy at the University of New Hampshire and kept my work life together over all these years. Liz knows all too well that I couldn't have done any of this without her. To Liz, I remain forever grateful.

Janet Flagg has worked behind the scenes for years mixing and pouring paint, packing classroom art materials kits, and making sure that teachers have access to quality materials at reasonable prices. Janet has played a key role in our efforts to get quality art materials into the hands of budding young artists and writers.

I would like to express my deepest gratitude to Dr. Dennis Meadows, who invited me to join his Institute at the University of New Hampshire in 1991 after reading about my "art residency" in the local paper. Dennis opened the door to a richly rewarding professional life I had never dreamed of having. His vision and belief in me launched my career and has sustained my journey all these years.

Then there are the students—hundreds of them—whose faces and images remain permanently imprinted in my visual memory and whose personal stories continue to inspire me. A few of their stories, along with some of their art and writing, appear sprinkled throughout this book. It is their lives, their creative work, and their honest reflections that have fueled my nearly two decades of inquiry and, to this day, dwell inside me. Occasionally, I hear their voices speaking to me. At this very moment, for instance, I hear the words of second-grader Chelsea as she reflected on *finally* finishing her book, "My dream come true was my book was all done and I was really excited for my book to be all done and I really wanted to read it." Then I hear the words of Gani, my eight-year-old friend from Uzbekistan who shared with me his big dreams for his book, "I think it is nice to make the book because I can show people of the world this book." To all my students, whose hard work has expanded their hopes and dreams, I offer my deepest appreciation. You have been my best teachers.

To my three daughters
Misa, Shana and Noami
each of whom in her own way
deepened my understanding
of the power of pictures

The Author

Beth Olshansky has spent the last two decades exploring the dynamic relationship between pictures and words with thousands of teachers and students across the United States and Canada, as well as within several U.S. commonwealths and territories. She is the developer of two proven art-and-literature-based approaches to writing: "Picturing Writing: Fostering Literacy Through Art" and "Image-Making Within The Writing Process." As founder and director of the Center for the Advancement of Art-Based Literacy at the University of New Hampshire, Beth continues to develop and refine these alternative art-based literacy models, conduct research, and offer onsite experiential teacher-training across the country as well as at the University of New Hampshire. To learn more about her work, visit www.picturingwriting.org.

About the DVD

I created a DVD to accompany this book because, as a visual and kinesthetic learner, I was convinced that I could not convey a visual process through words alone; I wanted to offer readers the whole picture.

The DVD was filmed in a third-grade classroom that was relatively new to art-based literacy. Our camera crew arrived on a day in late October, not long after I had begun working with the class. This was the students' third time to gather on the rug for a Literature Share prior to an art lesson. I purposely wanted to show viewers what the process might look like with a class relatively inexperienced in this way of working.

I also selected a class that contained a wide range of learners. Beyond the obvious ethnic diversity, the class of twenty-one students contained three English language learners, five students with IEPs (individualized education plans), and eight students on behavioral medications. There was also a fair amount of transience with nine students entering or leaving the class midyear. (I tell you this after a colleague viewed the DVD and remarked that I had obviously chosen an exceptional class to work with. The point is that this group of students *became* exceptional when given the tools they needed to be successful.)

In order to capture the rhythm and flow of Artists/Writers Workshop, the Overview follows one distinct set of art-and-literature-based mini-lessons from beginning to end—a single art strand and a single writing strand; the art you see and the writing you hear grew out of that one set of lessons. All the art and writing mini-lessons were filmed on this day (not the recommended way to work, but dictated by finances). The camera crew returned later in the year to finish filming students sharing their writing and reflecting on the process.

The DVD contains three chapters. The first chapter is a 28-minute overview of Artists/Writers Workshop. This overview takes you into the classroom to witness the process firsthand. The Overview contains chapter markers so you can click through to various sections (Literature Share, Modeling Session, Work Session, and Group Share) for purposes of a quick review. The best parts, in my opinion, are the students' reflections about the process, which serve as bookends to the piece. You will find them at the very beginning and the very end of the Overview. They say it all.

The other two chapters are purely instructional in nature. The Introduction to Watercolor on Wet Paper is the very first structured painting lesson I offer students following an opportunity to simply experiment with watercolor on wet and dry paper. This chapter on how to model watercolor on wet paper is about 3 minutes long and reflects the content in the second painting lesson in Chapter Nine. I always offer students an opportunity to become familiar with painting watercolor on wet paper before I introduce the more complex crayon resist process.

The final chapter of the DVD offers an introduction to crayon resist. During a 7-minute demonstration, I model how I introduce crayon resist to the class. Though short clips of this modeling session are included in the Overview, in this chapter, entitled Complete Crayon Resist Lesson, I show you the entire modeling session. You get to see it all.

My hope is that this narrated visual Overview (words and pictures together!) and the two demonstration art lessons, coupled with Chapter Nine in this book, will provide you with enough information to get started. I am eager for you to sample the process. You may witness some new and surprising pathways to literacy opening up for your students, particularly for those whom you consider your most challenging learners. Please note as you watch the DVD that while this class definitely included a wide range of learners, it is hard to identify students "at the low end of the spectrum." There is a reason for that. I hope that by the time you finish reading this book, you will understand why.

The
Power
of
Pictures

part one

The Foundation

1 Why Build Art into Literacy Learning?

Writing used to be hard for me, but now it is easy.
All I have to do is look at each picture [I made] and describe some things I see.
I listen to my words to see if they match with my story and they always do.

—David, Grade 2

If you are a teacher, I have no doubt you have met a student like David.

David usually spent most of the school day looking for reasons to get out of his seat. The pencil sharpener, the wastebasket, the water fountain, and the bathroom all provided predictable pathways through David's second-grade classroom and welcome excuses to roam. Writing time was the worst part of the day for David because it demanded he stay in his seat and focus his attention. He spent much of writing time each day fiddling with little pieces of folded paper inside his desk and glancing up at the clock. If he could only wait long enough, it would be time for recess.

"I hate to write," David once confided to his teacher. "The words fly out of my head before I can get them down on paper." Perceptive as this insight was, verbalizing it did not help David cope with the many challenges he faced each day. Sadly, at eight years old, David had already learned that teachers did not take kindly to him and that he was falling behind in school.

But this book is not another treatise bemoaning the fate of students who don't fit the mold required for success in school. David's story took an unexpected turn:

When David's teacher invited him to create his own portfolio of hand-painted textured papers, David became actively engaged. Later, when his teacher invited the class to "become detectives" and search for the story hidden within their portfolios of hand-painted papers, David stood apart from his peers—not for disruptive behavior but for his keen ability to discover images within his brightly colored, hand-painted papers.

David was the first to discover his story. A geometric design in a Plexiglas print reminded him of a window. He quickly cut it out and peered through it to search for the rest of his story. He spotted a swirling tornado in his blue marbleized paper. As soon as he cut out the tornado, freeing it from the page, the tornado took on a life of its own. Propelled by David's active body, the tornado spun around the classroom accompanied by great whooshing sounds.

David embodied his story-making process. As a visual, tactual, and kinesthetic learner, he constructed collage image after collage image, eagerly securing each animated shape to his sequence of pictures once he had "practiced each page," complete with movement and a wide range of sound effects. While David did not choose to write during his collage-making process, he enthusiastically rehearsed his story over and over again, collage image by collage image. With each retelling, his story grew in detail and description.

As his active fingers traced the edges of his collage shapes, descriptive language was literally at his fingertips. Holding a magenta and purple marbleized paper in his hand, he announced, "It seems like we're caught in a meteor shower. Huge rocks like pumpkins hit me from all sides. It's raining rocks." (See Color Plate A.) David ducked, his hands flying over his head to protect himself from the "dusty storm."

Through his repeated retellings, David was able to memorize his story so that the words no longer flew out of his head before he could get them down on paper. And should he forget, David had a concrete visual record of his thoughts glued down right in front of him in the brightly colored images he had fashioned.

Using these dynamic, concrete tools, David created a coherent and engaging story replete with vivid picture and word images. As he thumbed through the pages of his published book for the first time, he glanced up with tears in his eyes and said, "I didn't know I could do that good . . ."

For David, this experience of success was life-altering. Not only did he gain new respect from his teacher and his peers, he also discovered his own talents as a gifted crafter of story. From that point on, he developed a passion for creating stories driven by his important realization: "Writing used to be hard for me, but now it is easy. All I have to do is look at each picture and describe some things I see." Smiling, David added, "Now writing is my favorite part of school." David was one of the first students who, years ago, opened my eyes to the power of pictures to enhance literacy learning. The transformation that took place in David as a powerful writer, as an engaged learner, and as a self-respecting and respected human being stayed with me and fueled the deepening of my inquiry into the dynamic relationship between pictures and words. Since then, I have witnessed hundreds of students of all ages who, like David, were not well suited to our verbally oriented educational system, but who thrived when allowed to construct meaning and express themselves using the language of pictures.

Their experiences have resonated with me. As a visual and kinesthetic learner myself, I recognize the challenges these diverse learners face as they struggle to make their way through a system poorly designed to meet their learning needs. For nearly two decades, the faces, the personal challenges, and the successes of these students have stayed with me and spurred me on to continue to grow and refine my art-based approach to literacy learning.

Along the way, I began to notice something curious: it was not just the struggling readers and reluctant writers who benefited from participating in this alternative pathway to literacy learning. Instead, virtually all students found new and stronger voices as they learned to use visual tools to deepen their thinking and more fully express their ideas.

The Hidden Verbal Bias

In my early years of elementary school in the mid-1950s, I remember my father, an intellectual and avid reader, asking me who the "smart kids" were in school. I knew exactly what he meant: those kids who were good at the 3 R's: reading, writing, and 'rithmetic. But what about my other classmates, the ones who got D's and F's on their report cards but were amazing artists or skillful athletes? Even as a six- and seven-year-old I understood that many of these kids were in trouble.

And indeed, their frequent trips to the principal's office in elementary school often turned into detentions and suspensions in junior high, and to truancy and even more reckless behaviors in high school. Some of my elementary school classmates who struggled with reading and writing stopped coming to class altogether in high school. Those who did stay barely graduated. While my honors English and math classes did not include these students, I knew most of them well because they were in my art classes. It was the one time of day when their talent were recognized. I often wondered if the rest of their teachers knew about their extraordinary gifts.

While I too struggled with reading and writing early in my school career, I was fortunate. My parents had faith in my ability to learn. They treated me like the intelligent human being they knew I was, which allowed me to maintain my dignity and self-respect despite the daily challenges I faced. As a visual and kinesthetic learner, however, I lived every day with the deep disconnect between my inner world and the word-centered world of school. At times, I became very self-conscious about my failed attempts to learn how to read.

By the time I was in second grade, I was well aware that I was still not reading and most of my classmates were. Week after week, my parents would patiently walk with me down to our local bookmobile so I could pick out the most visually appealing picture books from along the bottom shelf of its musty book-lined walls.

My parents would read these books to me over and over again during the week. Then sometimes, if the book didn't have too many words, they would tell me it was my turn to read a page. Inevitably, I would stumble through the short text, my body tensing with every unfamiliar word, my stomach tied in knots.

Finally, deciding I'd had enough, I announced to my parents that they didn't have to read to me anymore; I had learned to read. In fact, I told them, I could read an entire book.

I sat down with them to prove it. Then, page by page, I proceeded to read the pictures, delivering a well-rehearsed rendition of the story. As a visual learner, I was quite good at picture reading. Somehow I thought I could fool my parents—after all, my words *sounded* like a real story. Apparently, it never occurred to me that because my parents knew how to read and I didn't, I would be found out. Such is the logic of an eight-year-old. Fortunately, my parents were kind enough to play along and chose not to embarass me.

This relatively inconsequential anecdote in the life and times of a struggling reader illustrates an important point: for young children, reading pictures comes as naturally as speaking. This ability to read pictures, to make meaning, seems to be programmed into our brains. Even young children can decode the meaning of pictures and encode meaning into pictures with ease, without ever being taught to do so. This is something most educators rarely consider.

My personal experience growing up as someone who learned differently (than the way things were taught), and the experience of watching my own three children (with their diverse learning strengths) go through our educational system, helped me years ago to recognize the intelligence of those who learn differently. Of course, I am not the only one who has arrived at this understanding. In *Envisioning Writing,* Janet

Olson (1992) shares her observations and poses critical questions: "Many children have problems with language. Is it because they are "learning disabled" or "reluctant writers"? Or is it because they aren't being taught the way they need to be taught? Children who think and learn visually process information through images instead of through words, and these children often have great difficulties succeeding in school" (p. 1). She reminds readers, "Nothing is wrong with children who are visual learners. They are simply different from verbal learners. Teachers need to understand and incorporate visual thinking and visual learning strategies into conventional teaching methods in order to make it possible for both types of learners to reach their full language potential" (p. 6).

While Howard Gardner's theory of multiple intelligences (1983) has served to broaden our understanding of human ability and to accept, at least in theory, the intelligence of those who "learn differently," we still struggle within our educational system to live this truth. In spite of the evidence linking visual learning styles to creativity, ingenuity, and even genius (West, 1991), our educational system continues to disregard the intelligence of those who learn best through nonverbal means.

What History Tells Us

In his book, *In the Mind's Eye*, Thomas West (1991) forces us to confront some disturbing truths about our educational system through his extensive research into the learning idiosyncrasies and educational experiences of many of the world's most creative and original thinkers. West presents a significant body of evidence that documents how, throughout history, many of the world's most original thinkers and greatest innovators experienced tremendous learning difficulties in school in areas such as reading, writing, spelling, speaking, calculating, and memorizing. West discovered that a vast number of these great thinkers displayed what he refers to as "some form of dyslexia" in the broadest sense of the term (*dys* meaning difficulty and *lexia* meaning words). Albert Einstein, Thomas Edison, Winston Churchill, and William Butler Yeats, for example, all exhibited tremendous difficulties learning how to read or write and suffered tremendous humiliation during their schooling. Albert Einstein had a terrible memory for words, which made the standard rote learning methods of his day intolerable. As difficult as it may be to imagine, one of Albert Einstein's teachers told his parents that he would never amount to anything.

Thomas Edison was also the victim of an educational system that collided directly with his learning needs. Tedious lectures and rote memorization drove Edison to develop his own set of unusual compensatory behaviors including "putting his body in perpetual motion in his seat." One of Edison's teachers told his parents that they should not bother sending him to school as he had no capacity to learn.

These stories are not anomalies. West cites dozens of cases in which students who struggled pitifully in school and were made to feel like hopeless outcasts ended up in their later lives being recognized for their genius and unequaled contributions to society.

What is even more interesting (and not surprising) is that investigation into the notebooks of these original thinkers reveals that their innovative ideas, whether new theories or great inventions, were developed in pictures first, not in words. Upon closer analysis, there is a significant body of evidence that documents that these individuals who suffered with dyslexia exhibited strengths as visual learners and that their strong visual abilities actually paved the way for the creative thinking that ultimately led to the development of the innovative body of work they each produced. West concludes that there is a vital link between visual thinking, creativity, and the ability to solve problems creatively. Sadly, our schools rarely recognize the keen intelligence of visual learners.

Today's Schools

If you happen to have been born a verbal learner, meaning that words are a natural and comfortable medium for you, you have been cut from the cloth that our educational system is designed to teach. That is, the way you think is aligned with the way instruction is delivered. This is particularly true regarding instruction in verbal skills such as reading and writing.

However, if you happen to have been born a visual, tactual, or kinesthetic learner, our educational system is not designed to support your learning needs. Reading and writing (typically delivered through straight verbal forms of instruction) may not come easily to you, and that puts you at risk for a number of related social, emotional, and academic challenges. Again, Olson (1992) warns ". . . such children are in danger—they don't progress well academically, they perform poorly on tests, and they often suffer from poor self-esteem" (p. 1). Often, diverse learners, are made to feel intellectually inferior in school—an unfortunate though common fate.

As long ago as the 1960s and 1970s, research documented that third-grade reading level can be used as a strong predictor for high school graduation (Kelly, Veldman, & McGuire, 1964; Howard & Anderson, 1978; Lloyd, 1978). Students who have not mastered basic reading skills by third grade are far more likely to become high school drop-outs than are those who successfully acquire basic reading skills. Thus acquiring essential literacy skills early in one's school career is particularly critical to success not only in school but also in later life as well.

Yet traditionally those students who learn differently (from the way we teach) are subjected to tedious drills and tested to death using the very language that has already proven, time and again, to be ineffective for their learning style. Our low-performing students have shown repeatedly that they do not learn effectively through traditional auditory and verbal means. The mandates of No Child Left Behind—and the threat of punitive measures for schools that do not make "Adequate Yearly Progress"—only make matters worse for the very students they are designed to help.

Often administrators' typical reaction to the legislation is to insist that teachers apply more so-called rigor to their teaching by using the very same straight verbal methods that have so clearly failed to reach those being targeted. Yet low-performing students are likely not performing to the best of their ability because we are not teaching them in the way they best learn. Furthermore, while every student has areas of relative strength and weakness, by focusing on the weaknesses of our low-performing students and ignoring their strengths, we do little to help them learn. Without intending to do so, we often end up aggravating their problems and further programming them for failure. We strip them of their self-confidence, their dignity, and their will to learn while ignoring their many gifts and talents.

Framing the Challenge

With the recognition of multiple intelligences, diverse learning styles, and multiple ways of knowing, educational theory has made important advances in the last quarter of a century. At least in theory, we now accept that students do not all learn the same way and that predominantly verbal methods are not the only valid approach to teaching and learning. We now recognize that there exists more than one way to develop and express ideas, or to construct meaning. With this recognition, the stage has been set for us to acknowledge that our schools have traditionally discriminated against nonverbal learners.

Hand in hand with this recognition of multiple intelligences and diverse learning styles comes the responsibility to consider how we can successfully reach *all our students*. All too often, classroom teachers remain uncertain as to how to put this sound theory into practice. This is especially true when it comes to teaching verbal skills such as reading and writing.

Even educators who clearly grasp the theory and have the best intentions are easily derailed by the tremendous pressures they face—pressures to meet state standards, to teach district-mandated curriculum, and to prepare students for standardized tests in order to meet the federal mandates established by No Child Left Behind. These pressures weigh heavily on educators, making it difficult to embed sound theory into daily teaching practices. With mounting pressure to teach to the test, it is extremely difficult to move beyond traditional straight verbal methods for teaching essential literacy skills. And yet the stakes have become even higher for those who learn differently, for their teachers, and for their school districts.

How Students Learn

In 1995, *Learning Magazine* published the research findings of Dr. Sue Teele, who conducted an inventory of where students' strengths lie, based on Howard Gardner's initial seven multiple intelligences (Brudnak, 1995). In a typical primary classroom of twenty-six students, Teele documented

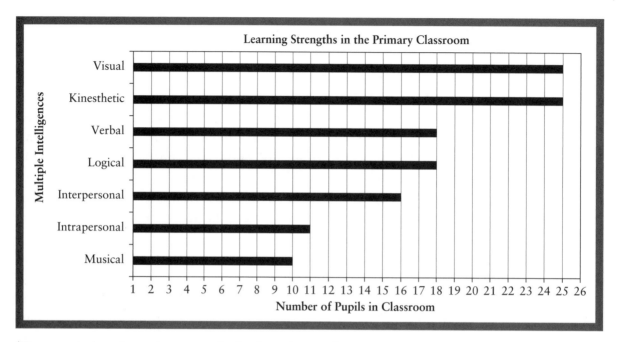

Figure 1.1.   Learning strengths in the primary classroom.
Source: Research by Dr. Sue Teele, 1995.

that twenty-five displayed strengths as visual and kinesthetic learners[1] (Figure 1.1). Only eighteen demonstrated strengths as verbal learners. That means that if you are a first-grade teacher teaching reading and writing the way you have been taught to teach reading and writing (through practice in reading and writing), approximately one-third of your students will be at a clear disadvantage (see Figure 1.1).

Teele's research revealed that students retain their visual and kinesthetic strengths all through elementary and middle school. Her study documented that after third grade, students' strengths as verbal learners actually diminish. Today, this phenomenon, is often referred to as "fourth-grade slump" (see Table 1.1).

These findings also correlate with research mentioned earlier, which documented that students who would later drop out of high school could be identified based on their third-grade reading levels. There is ample evidence that students must be given the opportunity to succeed early in their school career (Anderson, Hiebert, Scott, &

1. It can be assumed that tactual learners were grouped with the kinesthetic learners—those who learn best through hands-on experiences.

Table 1.1. How students learn through the grades

Dominant Strengths	K	First	Second	Third	Fourth	Fifth	Middle School
Visual	•	•	•	•	•	•	•
Verbal	•	•	•	•			
Kinesthetic	•	•	•	•	•	•	•
Intrapersonal	•						
Interpersonal				•	•	•	•
Musical					•	•	•
Mathematical	•	•	•				

Source: Research findings by Dr. Sue Teele, 1995.

Wilkinson, 1985; McPartland & Slavin, 1990). While this has been known for some time, and even though Howard Gardner's theory of multiple intelligences provides a framework for broadening the discussion about intelligence, many school systems remain locked into the traditional verbocentric notion of learning—particularly when it comes to teaching reading and writing. And yet we press on, driven by test preparation and assessment after assessment while ignoring this critical question: How does a classroom teacher teach verbal skills such as reading and writing to those who are not verbal learners? As educators, we continue to struggle to find our way.

Another Perspective on Visual Learners

In *Right-Brained Children in a Left-Brained World,* Jeffery Freed (a former teacher, now an educational therapist and consultant) contends that without exception, every student he has ever worked with who has been labeled as having Attention Deficit Disorder (ADD) or Attention Deficit/Hyperactivity Disorder (ADHD) is a visual and kinesthetic learner and right-brained thinker (Freed & Parsons, 1997).

Because these students don't function well within our very left-brained, verbally based educational system, they are labeled as deficient and made to feel inadequate as learners. They, like other visual, tactual, or kinesthetic learners, become victims of the hidden verbal bias within our educational system. Of course, the more we pressure diverse learners to "do it right" (that is, our way), the more resistant they grow to learning (our way), and the more they lose faith in their own abilities. Without intending to, we have created an educational system that tests students for a limited kind of intelligence (predominantly verbal-logical), identifies many of them as deficient (across the board and not just in this limited realm), and then dwells on the weaknesses thus revealed. This only compounds the challenges faced by those who do not fit into our verbocentric box.

Net of Exclusion

Freed is not alone in suggesting that most school administrators (those in the position of determining policy), and many classroom teachers (especially those who end up specializing in teaching reading and writing) are likely to be verbal learners. (This assumption is based on the fact that they have successfully risen up through the ranks of our verbally based educational system, and in the case of literacy experts, are often drawn to specialize in those areas where they themselves feel most accomplished.) Because these educators and administrators themselves are not visual learners, they find it difficult to understand or imagine what it is like to be a visual learner. Test developers, of course, are also most likely to be verbal learners.

West maintains that our educational system creates an unrecognized "net of exclusion" that serves to prevent diverse thinkers from successfully moving through the system and therefore prevents them from being placed in positions of authority or policymaking in their adult lives. He maintains that it is indeed rare, and often only the result of some chance event, for a visual or kinesthetic learner to reach a position of influence or authority—particularly one that dictates educational policy. Such learners are even less likely to wind up in a position that determines educational policy in the field of literacy learning. Given this, it is easy to understand how our schools have become designed to neglect our diverse learners.

The Visual Avenue to Verbal Learning

Counterintuitive as it may seem to teach verbal skills such as reading and writing through art, this approach makes sense when considered more closely. Pictures do not serve a merely decorative function; they are our first written language, both in the history of human culture and within the lifetime of each human being. The connection between art and writing, between the language of pictures and the language of words, is an ancient and natural one.

Embedded somewhere in our DNA, no matter what our race or culture may be, we are programmed to progress through the evolutionary stages of development of humankind beginning at conception and proceeding well beyond birth. This recapitulation includes retracing the evolutionary stages of written language. Beginning with making marks—in the mud, in the sand, on bedroom walls—as soon as children are old enough to hold a stick or a crayon, they discover their own power to alter a surface, to create. It becomes and remains a source of fascination and delight.

Young children intuitively understand the meaning of pictures long before they are taught how to read words on paper. Whether or not a well-meaning adult can "read" the pictures a child creates, the young artist can explain with confidence exactly what a particular drawing means. Children can also look at pictures created by others and read those pictures for meaning. Pictures are indeed a child's first written language, and one that children generally acquire on their own. Unlike writing (letters, words, and sentences), pictures are a language that does not have to be taught.

But what happens to this innate language of pictures once children enter elementary school? While teachers of very young children (kindergarten and first grade) encourage their emergent writers to draw to help them put their ideas down on paper (Routman, 1994), this practice is often discouraged as soon as students acquire the ability to write. In the name of not frittering away precious writing time, many elementary school teachers urge students to distance themselves from their natural language of pictures early in their school career. Given the diverse learning strengths students are now known to have, I believe this deliberate distancing from their first written language is shortsighted and ill-conceived. As educators, we are often in such a hurry to get to the "real work" of writing and reading (those skills that are tested) that we unknowingly sever an important lifeline to literacy learning. This is especially true for those students who are not naturally strong verbal learners.

Once we recognize that pictures are our first written language (both as a species and as individuals), we may begin to understand that taking away students' first language of pictures is akin to setting them adrift in a foreign sea. Pictures provide a natural language for all children, particularly for those who are visual or experiential learners, emergent writers, or struggling to learn a second language. Pictures provide a vital life raft for second-language learners, one that can make the difference between sinking or staying afloat. When we insist that emergent readers and writers—of any language—distance themselves from their natural language of pictures, we are not only taking away their life raft but also asking them to swim against the current. And we wonder why we are losing so many of our students along the way.

What are the implications of acknowledging these realities? Should educators just ignore students' learning difficulties? Or stop trying to teach students how to read and write at the first sign of difficulty? Absolutely not. However, it is essential that we break out of the verbocentric box imposed by our educational system and find ways to serve *all* learners, not just those fortunate enough to fit the system. I have witnessed time and again that struggling readers and reluctant writers rise to the occasion and produce quality work when they are given the tools they need to succeed. Showing students what they are capable of achieving when they apply the strengths they do possess, can in itself be a powerful life lesson.

A More Democratic Way

Most teachers can recall a student (past or present) who could spend hours creating extremely detailed and precise line drawings, yet struggle with basic reading and writing skills. These students are common in our classrooms. If we care to pay attention, these students are telling us (showing us) *how* they learn, yet we often do not listen. We need to ask ourselves what we are doing to our children by ignoring these important clues to unlocking literacy learning.

Our educational system continues to identify and label these students as deficient when in truth it is the system that is deficient. Thomas West (1991) believes, as I do, that our system is failing great numbers of students who become convinced of their inability to learn simply because our teaching methods are not aligned with the way they learn. He maintains that these very students "who think differently" may well hold the inner capacity to discover innovative solutions to today's problems, if only their teachers were able to recognize and respect their intelligence and support their unique learning strength.

When I think about all the human gifts that go unrecognized, when I think about all the students I have known who have become discouraged learners, because our educational system is unable to serve their needs or recognize their talents, I am deeply troubled. We should and can do better. We can begin by recognizing the invisible form of discrimination that exists within our schools; only then can we begin to build a truly democratic educational system, one that serves to honor *all students,* not just the verbal learners.

We need to look to our students' strengths to show us the way.

2 Bringing Words and Pictures Together

A New Model

"I learned that after you paint your pictures, it is much easier to write because you have all the details right in front of you."

—Grayson, Grade 3

Everyday speech is full of reminders of the power of pictures to communicate. When we say, "a picture is worth a thousand words" or "that painting *speaks* volumes," we acknowledge the ability of pictures to convey meaning much as verbal language does. Conversely, "I *see* what you mean," acknowledges that the link between the verbal and the visual goes both ways in conveying meaning.

Additionally, we all recognize that effective writers have mastered the art of painting pictures in the reader's mind, and effective readers are able to visualize what they are reading. Remarking that "the pictures *tell* a story" or that "the words *paint* a picture" acknowledges the complementary nature of pictures and words. Pictures really can serve the verbal function of *telling* or *speaking,* and words can serve the visual function of *creating a picture.*

In *Word Painting: A Guide to Writing More Descriptively,* Rebecca McClanahan (1999) draws many parallels between the art of painting and the art of writing. She writes, "Description is, in effect, *word painting*" (p. 7). She later expands upon this notion: "Description can provide the palette for gradations in mood and tone. Dip your brush in one description and the sky darkens; in another and the sun breaks through" (p. 11). She reminds us that the work of the painter and the work of the writer both begin with careful observation. Driven by the desire to capture a visual image on paper, the artist observes deeply and then tries to represent both vision and mood through the layering of visual elements. The writer looks deeply as well, sifting through and layering words to capture image, sound, smell, taste, and texture. Through deep observation, "the most common things can yield startling surprises" (p. 15).

Such is the case when a lesson brings together art and writing, inviting the mind of the artist and the mind of the writer to dwell, even coexist, inside us. With the option of seeing "with two minds" and intertwining two languages to capture that vision, our power of expression is greatly enhanced. A well-crafted picture book exemplifies this dynamic marriage between pictures and words.

Two Complementary Languages

The right-brain/left-brain dichotomy, born of experiments performed in the late 1960s on epileptic patients whose left and right hemispheres had been surgically severed (Sperry, 1968), was later found to be overly simplistic. At that time, the left hemisphere was thought to govern all sequential, logical, analytical, verbal thinking while the right hemisphere was thought to govern more intuitive processing and nonverbal, holistic thinking. While there remains some truth to these distinctions, researchers now recognize that the brain functions in a much more complex and sophisticated manner, with involvement of both hemispheres in most activities (Caine & Caine, 1994).

For example, someone who performs the verbal tasks of reading or writing must create mental pictures in the process. Likewise, an artist may well plan out a painting using analytic skills. That said, it is still clear that most classroom activities in schools today are dominated by logical, analytical, verbal thinking, while the capacity to think in more intuitive, holistic ways remains virtually untapped, except during the occasional arts "specials." Schools that follow this pattern are under-utilizing students' available brain power, which is particularly unfortunate for those whose strengths lie in the nonverbal realm.

While reading and writing call for very complex mental processing that involves a certain amount of thinking in pictures, the act of engaging in these processes is undeniably linear in nature. To read, the eyes move from left to right along defined lines of words and sentences. Readers sound out individual letters or letter blends and then combine them to read individual words; they piece together words to read sentences; and they string together sentences to read paragraphs. Writers must arrange letters, words, sentences, and paragraphs in a sequential, linear fashion to be read and understood. (When words are written in a nonlinear fashion, scattered on a page—like word magnets on a refrigerator door—readers see this very differently and attempt to make sense of it as "artistic expression.") In both reading and writing, readers move from parts to whole (letters to words to sentences to paragraphs) as they make meaning.

By contrast, reading pictures or creating art is generally a nonlinear activity. Readers of a picture take in the whole image before the eye wanders to the picture's various parts to digest their full meaning and contribution to the whole. In creating a picture, the artist often (though not always) envisions the whole image before creating various parts. The two distinct mediums of pictures and words engage their audience in very different kinds of thinking: more sequential parts-to-whole thinking when working with words and nonsequential, nonlinear whole-to-parts (to whole again) thinking in picture-reading or picture-making.

Universal Language

Pictures can also serve as a universal language, one that is accessible no matter what language one speaks. Not so with the language of words. In fact, the language of words can be specific to each culture, each country, and sometimes each region, with local dialects creating yet another layer of distinction. When I worked with Yup'ik teachers in Alaska, I learned that one school district (admittedly, the size of the state of Ohio) was home to seven different Yup'ik dialects spoken among its twenty-one villages, with some dialects so distinct that their speakers have difficulty communicating in Yup'ik with those from other villages in the same school district. By contrast, the language of pictures needs no translation.

Serve Complementary Functions

The relationship between pictures and words can be summarized simply. Although these two languages are both used to make meaning, they function very differently. Yet clearly they serve to complement each other: pictures, a visual medium, can perform the verbal function of *telling* a story; words, a verbal medium, can perform the visual function of *painting* a picture. Using both languages expands our capacity to think in new and interesting ways.

Theoretical Background

By defining students as both writers *and* artists and engaging them in the combined crafting of pictures and words, we invite them to contribute much more of their individual potential to the thinking and learning process. With this dual-language approach, students engage several of the intelligences that Howard Gardner identified in his 1983 book, *Frames of Mind: The Theory of Multiple Intelligences* (linguistic, logical-mathematic, spatial, bodily-kinesthetic, musical, interpersonal, and intrapersonal, plus an eighth added in 1999, naturalistic). In addition, the learning environment established by the combined art and writing approach is supported by the work of several other learning theorists, including Geoffrey and Renate Nummela Caine, Lev Vygotsky, and Albert Bandura. Beyond these supporting theoretical frameworks and the best practices that I will describe later in this chapter, two research studies on this particular approach to art-based writing have been completed, the results of which appear in Appendix A.

Brain-Based Learning

In *Making Connections: Teaching and the Human Brain,* Geoffrey and Renate Nummela Caine apply critical findings from the field of neuroscience to educational theory and practice. According to the Caines, these findings challenge previously accepted notions that the brain naturally separates emotion from cognition, the implications of which shine a light on the importance of personal engagement and motivation in learning. To be effective, learning must be meaningful to the learner. Thus, offering a visual, tactual or kinesthetic learner the opportunity to engage in reading and writing activities that have picture-making at their core will greatly enhance student engagement and motivation, and thus student learning. Now add a progression of art-and-literature-based mini-lessons designed around specific literary or literacy goals to the mix and teachers will foster high motivation, high engagement, and high learning.

As advocates for deepening understanding of what constitutes effective teaching practice and powerful learning based on current brain research, the Caines offer a wealth of guidelines for teachers to enhance learning in the classroom. Among them, they recommend establishing classrooms designed around the principles of orchestrated immersion in meaningful projects over time, relaxed alertness to support creative thinking, and active processing of the experience to deepen students' understanding through reflection. Their in-depth brain-based analysis of how students learn is well worth reading. Their recommendations for optimum learning are well aligned with practices integral to the art-based writing workshop process described in this book.

Vygotsky's Zone of Proximal Development

Socio-psycholinguist Lev Vygotsky theorized that all children have a "zone of proximal development" (1978, p. 86). By this he means a range of activities or tasks that they can perform when supported by others but could not perform independently. According to Vygotsky, when participating in lessons within their "zone of proximal development," students will eventually gain the ability to perform these tasks on their own after initially receiving help. Vygotsky also maintained that this zone of learning will keep advancing for students as they continue to expand their range of abilities.

With the regular infusions of literature-based mini-lessons and classroom modeling sessions coupled with ongoing group shares described in this book, teachers who follow the guidelines I outline will continually expand students' zone of proximal development as their students are regularly encouraged to apply new understandings of both art and writing concepts to their work. Tasks that may at first require teacher guidance for students to perform soon become internalized skills as students eagerly engage in the process and take ownership and pride in their work.

Self-Efficacy Beliefs

Social psychologist Albert Bandura (1997) contends that human beings' level of motivation, affective state, and actual performance are based more on what they believe they can accomplish than on what their objective capacity may be. Self-efficacy (belief in one's personal capability) is a key component to the workings of the process described in this book.

Defined as artists and writers and given the task of creating their own quality picture books, students study the work of professionals from an insider's perspective. This positions them to see themselves as part of an inner circle of soon-to-be professionally published artists and writers. They are eager to learn from the masters. (Note I prefer not to refer to students as *author/illustrators* because that term implies that the art merely illustrates the existing text rather than driving the story as is the case when pictures are created before the writing.)

With a steady stream of focused, art-and-literature-based mini-lessons, whole-group modeling sessions, shares, and scaffolded instructional practices tailored to meet the needs of students with a range of learning styles and abilities, students have the support they need to produce quality work. When they see what they are truly capable of producing using two languages (pictures and words), they naturally come to believe in themselves and their abilities. This only further enhances their confidence and belief in their own capabilities. First grader Sarah summed up self-efficacy when she reflected on the completion of her beautifully handcrafted collage book: "At first, when you first told us we were going to make books, I didn't think I could do it but then I just believed in myself and realized it was very easy."

It is worth mentioning that self-efficacy theory applies to teachers as well. Many teachers come to my experiential workshops convinced that they "can't draw a straight line." After being led through a progression of simple experiential art and writing lessons (very similar to the ones students are offered in the classroom), they soon discover that, much to their surprise, with some basic instruction, they can produce artwork they feel good about and quality writing. They also discover just how vital the art-making process can be to developing their ideas and accessing descriptive language. Teachers leave the workshop excited about the new tools they have acquired, which they will use in their classrooms to tap into the greater potential within every student. They soon shift their focus to believing in the process and ultimately they come to believe in themselves as facilitators as they witness their students—even their reluctant learners—respond to the process.

Redefining Pictures as a Language for Learning

It actually can be quite liberating to acknowledge what many of our diverse learners have been trying to tell us for years: that pictures are a powerful tool for thinking and recording ideas. When we recognize the power of pictures and choose to treat the language of pictures and the language of words as *equal, parallel,* and *complementary* languages for learning, we make a monumental paradigm shift. This single insight represents a powerful and critical divergence from current thought on supporting literacy learning in the classroom. This core shift in beliefs holds within it the power to revolutionize teachers' practice and students' learning.

Pictures and Words as Equal Languages

Once pictures and words are recognized as equal partners in literacy learning, it's no longer necessary to abide by conventional thinking whereby students must write before they illustrate their stories. (Note that the term *illustrate* perpetuates this conventional way of thinking by its very definition: "to provide explanatory or decorative pictures to accompany printed, spoken, or electronic text.")

If you truly believe that pictures and words are equally valid languages for developing, expressing, and recording ideas, you are free to rethink how you can support your students in creating quality writing. You can move beyond traditional practices that insist that students complete their writing ("the real work") before they illustrate their stories ("the decorative frosting on the cake"). You can also step back and observe how your students learn best and then establish classroom practices that truly support their literacy learning. Unfortunately, teachers are often so focused on moving students away from their natural language of pictures that they overlook the obvious: how the language of pictures can be enlisted to support writing instruction and enhance reading and writing practice. Once you recognize this as a possibility, a monumental transformation can occur not only in the way you think about art and the role it can serve in informing writing but also in your understanding of how you can maximize and tailor the use of art to teach the key elements of writing.

Equal, Parallel, and Complementary Languages

The study of quality picture books reveals many parallels between the languages of pictures and words. These parallels make it possible to teach key elements of writing, deepening students' understanding through the use of visual as well as verbal means. When you do this, you will find that you are able to reach a wide range of learners. Beyond learning to analyze how artists and writers make meaning using the distinct tools of their crafts, students become aware of how these dual languages complement and enhance each other in meaning making, thus offering fuller power of expression.

To fully comprehend this notion, it is essential to set aside any verbocentric beliefs about the key elements of story—especially the belief that the key elements of a story (setting, mood, character, problem, solution, and ending) are established solely through the language of words. In effective picture books, all these elements are conveyed by the pictures as well. Indeed, as mentioned in the Preface, it is possible to teach all these literary elements through the language of pictures.

For example, developing a sense of setting in a picture book or introducing the characters can be accomplished not only by words but also by the details within the pictures. It is interesting to analyze how authors and illustrators separately establish these key literary elements using their own distinct languages to convey meaning. The study becomes even more interesting as you become more aware of the potentially powerful marriage of these two forms of expression: how pictures and words work together to more fully express what each alone simply cannot fully convey.

Beyond Illustration: Defining Students as Artists and Writers

Moving beyond the more typical practices within a writing workshop (of writing and then illustrating existing text), the process described here is built on the belief that if *all students* are to become enthusiastic and capable writers, their teachers must reach out to them using languages they *all* understand. Given children's natural affinity for meaning making by both creating and reading pictures, it makes sense to expand the parameters of a writing workshop to include the language of pictures as a central tool for meaning making—beyond the currently accepted practice limited to working with emergent writers.

Rather than defining students primarily as authors and assigning them the job of crafting text, I believe that it is in the best interest of students and teachers to define students as artists as well as authors and engage them in the study and creation of quality picture books—from an insider's perspective. Allow me to explain how my experience has brought me to this conclusion.

Evolution of a New Model

My personal investigation into the relationship between art and writing began nearly two decades ago when one of my own children showed signs of having difficulty learning how to read and write. As a new mother (and one who didn't want to appear overly anxious), I tried my best to ignore my daughter's struggles, hoping that in time the problem would just go away. Time, in this case, did not prove to be the solution. By third grade, she was still having difficulty. Even worse, she became aware that her friends were reading with ease. Her self-esteem began to plummet.

Determined to do what I could to shore up her self-esteem, I decided to involve her more in the activities she did enjoy. (Of course, generally we enjoy those activities we have a natural affinity for.) That summer, I decided to take advantage of my daughter's zest for painting and offered a book illustration workshop on my back porch for neighborhood children. It was then that I noticed that with paintbrush in hand, my daughter was able to access imaginative ideas and descriptive language that were otherwise not available to her. With each new painting, rich sensory description seemed to be literally at her fingertips. The difference between the writing she produced while looking at one of her paintings and the writing she produced while staring at a blank piece of lined paper was profound.

I also noticed that she was not the only young writer on my back porch who preferred to develop stories through pictures. When given the choice, most of these children (ages five through twelve) chose to create their stories by making their pictures first. These observations whetted my curiosity and launched what has turned into a nearly two-decade-long inquiry into the rich relationship between pictures and words.

Early Thinking

When I first began exploring the relationship between art and writing in the classroom, Barbara Rynerson's first- and second-grade students had already been introduced to the key elements of story through picture book study. Barbara had chosen Eric Carle as the author/illustrator for the month of September. Invited into the classroom "to develop an illustration component to the writing process," I decided to support their literature study by having the students create their own portfolios of hand-painted papers. I then modeled how to construct a collage out of these hand-painted textured papers just like Eric Carle does. When it was time for these budding young artists and writers to begin their own stories, I made the following announcement: "Today, we are going to begin *working* on our stories." I purposely did not instruct students to write first or make pictures first, as I was eager to observe their choices. Of the twenty-three students, all but one chose to make pictures first rather than write first. This finding precisely mirrored the later results of Dr. Sue Teele's 1995 research mentioned in Chapter One (Brudnak, 1995), in which twenty-five out of twenty-six primary students exhibited strengths as visual and kinesthetic or tactual learners.

Because twenty-two out of twenty-three first- and second-grade students chose to construct their sequence of collage images before they wrote their stories, I was able to eavesdrop on their conversations as they were cutting and pasting. I noticed immediately how engaged they became in crafting their stories. Their oral language was unusually descriptive as they talked in detail to one another about their story ideas. I also noticed that the writing that grew from making their collage images first was extraordinarily rich in detail and description. Students' story ideas were also far more imaginative than the ones the same group had produced just a few weeks earlier, and the resulting writing also shifted from the "bed-to-bed" personal narratives typical of their age group to more fiction.

While I witnessed these exciting transformations occurring in the classroom, I wanted to be careful not to replace the existing educational bias (favoring the verbal learner) with another (favoring a different learning style). Because of this, despite my observations regarding the success of students who chose to create their pictures first, I publicly espoused the notion that students should work "according to their individual learning styles." That made perfect sense to me. In fact, in the Heinemann videotape I produced in 1992, *Children as Authors, Children as Illustrators: The Whole Story,* I clearly state that students are free to "make their pictures first, write first, or weave back and forth between the two." Despite my personal observations to the contrary, I strove to be egalitarian in my thinking.[2]

I continued to make these public pronouncements even though, year after year, I observed that students who made their pictures first made the greatest advances in their writing. Their stories were far more imaginative and their writing was far richer in detail and description than stories produced by the students who chose to write first. This observation was even validated by the research study cited in Appendix A that involved 377 first and second graders, half of whom used collage and made their pictures first and half of whom were following a more traditional writing workshop format. Still, I worked hard to maintain what I thought was an objective, "balanced" perspective.

---

2. That video is now available through the Center for the Advancement of Art-Based Literacy at the University of New Hampshire, along with a teachers manual and set of professionally published student-made collage books.

Then, in 1995 (five years into my investigation), I was confronted by a group of eighteen K–5 teachers who, at the end of a three-month collage-based writing project, gathered to share their observations. One by one, each teacher observed that she had noticed that the students who crafted their collage images first produced better writing. As I nodded in agreement after each confirmation of my own observations, several teachers blurted out in unison, "Why didn't you tell us!" It was then that I had to admit that, while my observations matched theirs, I had made a conscious decision to avoid making recommendations that seemed to promote yet another learning bias. Finally, backed by the observations of so many teachers, I began to speak my truth: I believe that students who make pictures first have an advantage over those who write first. I believe that in most cases this is true even for students who are comfortable crafters of words.

The End Result: Artists/Writers Workshop

Fast-forwarding to the present, after years of thoughtful and intensive exploration in hundreds of K–8 classrooms, I have developed what I call "Artists/Writers Workshop." This model seamlessly integrates quality literature into every art and writing mini-lesson, each designed with a clear literary purpose. Artists/Writers Workshop provides a simple four-step format for offering a systematic progression of mini-lessons complete with concrete visual, tactual, and kinesthetic tools to support diverse learners at each and every stage of the writing process. The workshop model includes daily opportunities for all students to be honored for the strengths they possess while inviting them to enter a carefully crafted pathway into literacy learning that calls upon those strengths.

Within Artists/Writers Workshop, students become engaged in a detailed and systematic study of both text and illustrations. Using quality picture books as mentor texts, students learn from the masters as they become immersed in creating their own quality picture books. They study in depth the writer's and illustrator's craft as well as how the languages of pictures and words work together to tell the whole story. They learn how authors and illustrators weave together the parallel and complementary languages of words and pictures to express meaning and establish mood.

This opens the door to a whole new level of inquiry and engagement—which is of particular importance to students with little natural affinity for words. In fact, for struggling readers and reluctant writers, pictures may well be their only viable avenue to understanding the key elements of story.

Students also come to understand that rather than being part of a laborious exercise, words can make their pictures "come alive." They learn how to use their pictures to access descriptive language and become discerning crafters of words. Once words are something students can craft for their own purposes—a source of strength and pride rather than struggle and humiliation—their relationship with words transforms, as does the entire arena of literacy learning.

As students gain access to multiple modes of thinking, they are able to engage in writing—and, as it turns out, in reading too—from a position of strength and enthusiasm according to their individual learning styles. Teachers can use the Artists/Writers Workshop process with materials and subject matter of their own choice, weaving it into a variety of lessons or ongoing units of study. The chapters in Part Two present the process in detail, and include sample mini-lessons that can be used both as is to introduce the process to your students, or as a basis for designing other lessons. The companion DVD offers a real-life peek into the classroom to observe Artists/Writers Workshop in action. Artists/Writers Workshop provides a thoughtfully designed literature-based approach to writing that involves four steps:

Artists/Writers Workshop

+ Literature Share/Discussion
+ Modeling Session
+ Work Session
+ Group Share

1. *Literature Share/Discussion.* Every Artists/Writers Workshop begins by sharing a piece of quality literature (most often a picture book) selected for a particular purpose. A facilitated discussion follows that serves to draw students' attention to a particular aspect of the book depending on the objective

of the lesson. The sharing and discussion may focus on the pictures, on the words, or on how pictures and words work together to tell the whole story.

2. *Modeling.* Following the Literature Share/Discussion, the teacher models an art or writing process, incorporating students' observations made during the previous discussion and students' suggestions during the modeling session. As the teacher walks students through an art or writing process, the teacher solicits input, posing questions and selecting responses that generally serve to further the purpose of that particular lesson. Together, the class and teacher co-create a piece of art or a piece of writing as students receive explicit instruction and a "dry run" as a whole group before working independently on their own art or writing.

3. *Work Session.* Students work individually on their own art and writing, infused with new understandings that grew out of the Literature Share/Discussion and the teacher's explicit instruction during the Modeling Session.

4. *Group Share.* Individual students are invited to share their work (art or art and writing) with the class, placing their pictures in a special "Artists Frame" that serves to honor and enhance the work. During an art share, students learn how to read their pictures for detail and description; during a writing share, they read the writing created to accompany the picture. With a painting placed in the Artists Frame, writing is always viewed in relation to the art that inspired it. Only a few students are invited to share each day. I recommend that teachers maintain a class list of who has shared in order to make sure that everyone has an opportunity to share.

Organized around units of study, the Artists/Writers Workshop format provides an overarching framework for delivering ongoing writing and visual literacy instruction that honors and celebrates diversity within the classroom. Because students find the process so engaging, it is user-friendly for teachers as well—fostering an engaged community of learners. Cycling regularly through this simple four-step sequence of activities serves to establish a focused and dynamic learning community.

Chapter Seven addresses these four components of Artists/Writers Workshop in more detail and a comprehensive overview is provided in the companion DVD.

The Driving Force: Transmediation

Students engaged in Artists/Writers Workshop find themselves moving naturally between the language of pictures and the language of words. This allows them to experience an often unrecognized phenomenon: the power of transmediation.

Transmediation is defined as the act of recasting or translating meaning from one sign system to another. In this context, *sign systems* refer to the many ways we create and share meaning: (written) language, art, music, drama, movement, mathematics (Berghoff, Borgmann, and Parr, 2003). Marjorie Siegel (1995) maintains that the very act of recasting or translating meaning from one sign system to another increases opportunities for generative and reflective thought. Transmediation offers a powerful tool for thinking and learning.

Within Artists/Writers Workshop, students move back and forth between the language of pictures and the language of words. They gain access to the rich and diverse thought processes unique to each specific language. They also gain a second language with which to generate, develop, and express their ideas. The experience of transmediation serves to deepen students' thinking as they engage in the process of decoding and encoding meaning in both languages.

Additionally, I have noticed that when the language of pictures is offered as the first language for thinking and developing ideas, students who then write have already experienced a tremendous amount of rich visual thinking. The language of pictures provides a very concrete and dynamic core language for thinking and developing ideas before any writing takes place. It nourishes the mind and enriches thinking.

While this happens for virtually every student who participates in Artists/Writers Workshop, the power of transmediation was never so clear as it was when I observed Jamie, a first grader, create her collage story, *Someone Special* (1995). Jamie spent day after day immersed in constructing her sequence of collage images from the hand-painted papers she had created. Though most of her classmates were eager to talk about their pictures when invited, Jamie was not. Whenever I approached her to ask how she was doing, she refused to take her eyes off her work and would simply reply, "Fine." Her body language was clear. It said, "I am busy. Leave me alone." One day, I persisted, "Jamie, could you tell me about your pictures?" She looked up with her big soulful eyes and said, "Oh, I couldn't possibly do that. It is much too complicated." I decided to leave Jamie alone and not bother her anymore. Two days later, Jamie began to write to her sequence of carefully crafted collage images. The first two pages are shown in Figure 2.1. The collage images that inspired this writing can be viewed in Color Plates B and C.

As you can see, Jamie managed to put words to her big ideas after being quietly immersed in a process that allowed her to think deeply as well as move freely back and forth between pictures and words. While Jamie was a very capable first-grade writer before she began this collage process, never before had her language been so rich or her thinking so sophisticated. While Jamie's first draft was indeed amazing, when she read over her words, she noticed that she had written nearly the same sentence twice on the first page. Jamie crossed out the repeated sentence and then went on to make a few minor revisions to her text as she prepared her story for publication (Cragnoline, 1995).

In reflecting on Jamie's experience crafting her story, I believe that two factors should be taken into account when considering the amazing transformation of this first grader's writing. First, Jamie was working in a particularly rich art medium, which I discuss in more detail in Chapter Four. Second, because she was encouraged to develop her ideas in pictures first and then translate that meaning into words, I believe she experienced the power of transmediation. As Jamie worked to capture the meaning of her collage images in words, I believe that transmediation served to deepen her thinking by activating areas of the brain rarely engaged during the typical school day. I believe that transmediation, coupled with this particular art medium, encouraged more sophisticated thinking than this first grader had previously been able to access as she made meaning in one very dynamic medium and then translated that meaning into another.

Before I discovered the term *transmediation,* for years I viewed the powerful and surprising work I had observed coming from some of the most challenged or youngest of writers as a "kind of magic" that

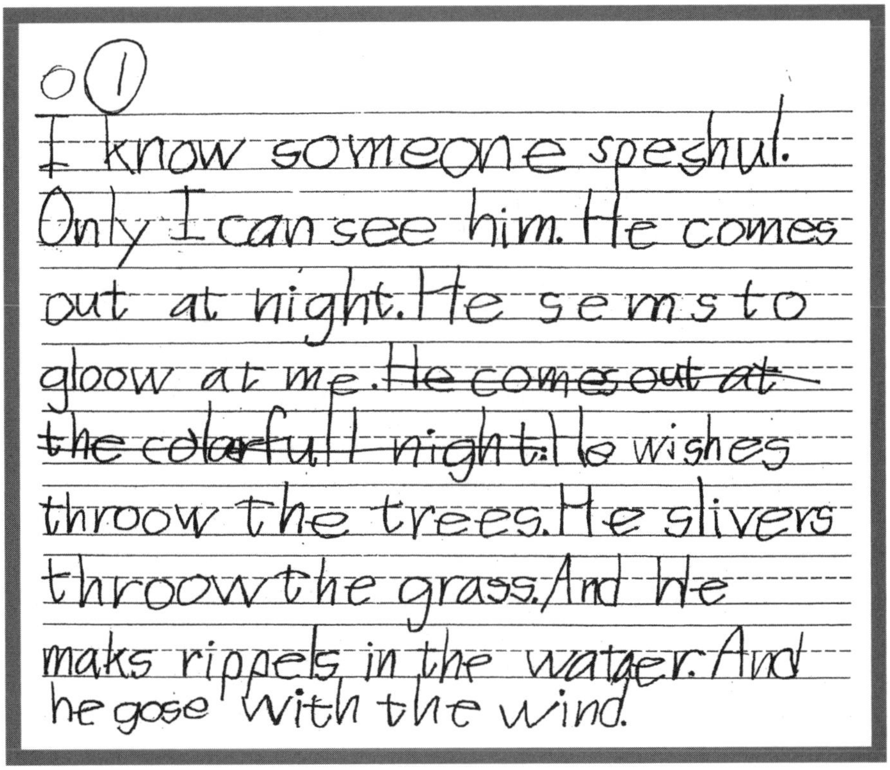

o (1)

I know someone speshul.
Only I can see him. He comes
out at night. He sems to
gloow at me. He comes out at
the colorfull night. He wishes
throow the trees. He slivers
throow the grass. And he
maks rippels in the water. And
he gose with the wind.

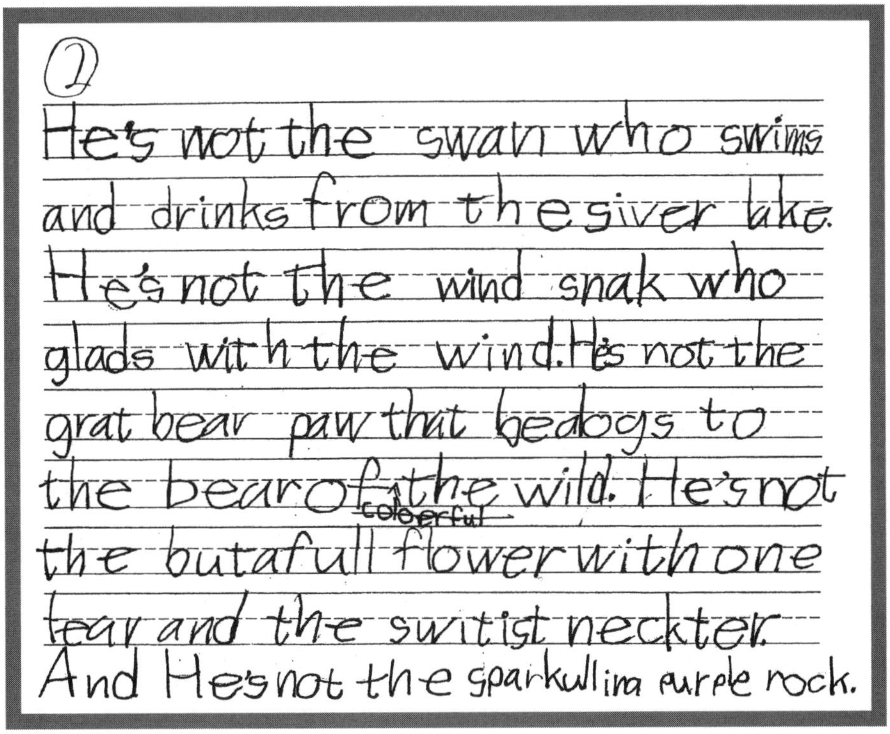

(2)

He's not the swan who swims
and drinks from the siver lake.
He's not the wind snak who
glads with the wind. He's not the
grat bear paw that bedoys to
the bear of the wild. He's not
the butafull flower with one
fear and the switist neckter.
And He's not the sparkullira purple rock.

Figure 2.1.   The first two pages of Jamie's story.

was occurring in the classroom. I now understand that this magic is the transformative power of transmediation.

Given the definition of transmediation—the recasting meaning from one sign system to another—readers may wonder why I don't include discussion of the more traditional move from words to pictures. Technically this too, would be considered a form of transmediation. The answer is quite simple: if we are interested in improving students' writing, the rich thinking that occurs during the picture-making process (*before* writing) is key. If students write first and then illustrate their writing, the thinking that occurs during their picture-making process will not impact their writing.

That said, it is difficult to fully grasp the power of transmediation without experiencing it. This account from another first-grade participant in Artists/Writers Workshop may help to shed further light on this phenomenon.

One mid-winter's day in New Hampshire after listening to Sadie and the Snowman, *six-year-old Chris sat down to draw his own snowman with crayons: three big circles stacked on top of each other. Inspired by the story, he then drew a big orange carrot for a nose, big brown cookies for the eyes, and a stick of red licorice for the smile. Then, with his crayons, he proceeded to draw an unusual brown and black striped hat on top of the snowman's head. He filled his remaining page with giant orange and white snowflakes, and with a pale orange crayon, he added a large crescent moon. Then he painted a quick watercolor wash over his picture to create the night sky. (See Color Plate D.) Later that day, Chris sat down to write to his picture: "One quiet and silent night, a raccoon sat on my snowman's head. A white owl hooted in a whisper. The moon smiled. The snowflakes fell more quietly than ever before. Drooom went the clock. The clock struck midnight and the stars sprinkled away."*

When Chris read his piece to the class (with his painting placed in the Artists Frame), his teacher asked him how he was ever able to come up with such wonderful words. Chris simply shrugged and then added, "I just don't know what happens. Whenever I go to Artists/Writers Workshop, all sorts of good stuff just pops into my head."

This first-grade explanation captures the essence of the experience of transmediation: "I just don't know what happens. All sorts of good stuff just pops into my head." While Chris could not articulate exactly how he came up with his imaginative ideas and wonderful words, he did understand one thing: Whenever he "goes to Artists/Writers Workshop," fuller power of expression is literally at his fingertips.

The power of the experience of transmediation cannot be conveyed in words alone, even through stories such as Jamie's and Chris'; it must be experienced to be fully understood. Please try to seek out an opportunity to experience this powerful phenomenon either by creating a picture and then writing to it as described in Chapter Nine and illustrated on the DVD, or by participating in a workshop designed to offer that experience.

Expanding on Best Practices

The workshop format and lessons described in this book grew out of keen observation of the creative process, deep listening, and the input of many veteran writing process teachers at a variety of grade levels. But the resulting approach embodies more than the results of trial and error, however successful; the process as it has evolved is well grounded in educational theory and current knowledge about best practices.

The original concept grew out of the writing workshop first articulated by Donald Graves in the early 1980s. Writing workshop defines students as authors and provides them with opportunities to move through the writing process (pre-writing, rehearsal, drafting, revising, and publication) on a regular basis. Writing workshop works well for some students, particularly for those who are comfortable working with words. Unfortunately, that describes only a subset of our student population. Expanding upon writing workshop, Artists/Writers Workshop defines students as artists as well as authors, thus appealing to students with a broader range of learning styles and strengths. It gives students visual tools at each and every stage of the writing process, and often kinesthetic tools as well. Pre-writing, rehearsal, drafting, and even revision are all approached in pictures before attempting to address these stages of writing in words—allowing students to use the language of pictures, which virtually all of them find engaging (even those who work easily with words). The process also ensures that students will experience the benefits of transmediation.

Embedded within Artists/Writers Workshop is the best practice of utilizing quality literature as *mentor texts*—texts worthy of deep study. Ralph Fletcher and JoAnn Portalupi (1998) recommend the use of picture books to study the writers' craft for students of all ages—including high school students. Katie Wood Ray and Lisa Cleaveland (2004) talk about the importance of reading like a writer, from an insider's perspective, and suggest the use of picture books as mentor texts for students as young as first grade. "Writers read differently than other people do. Writers notice and think about how texts are written, in addition to what texts are about. They can't help but notice; it's a habit of mind they adopt when they come to think of themselves as writers" (Wood Ray, 2004, p. 15).

This immersion in quality literature and students learning how to read like a writer represents a great advance for the writing process—yet I believe this "habit of mind" shouldn't end there. When students learn to see themselves as writers *and* artists, they begin to *read like a writer* and to *see like an artist* as they engage in studying picture books, analyzing and emulating these mentor texts, and creating their own carefully crafted picture books. Within Artists/Writers Workshop, the use of mentor texts goes far beyond the more traditional study of written text to include the study of the illustrations in picture books as well. Defined as artists and writers and indeed as crafters of their own quality picture books, students naturally become engaged in the study of the language of pictures *and* the language of words. As students embrace the study of pictures and words in quality picture books, they come to understand the fuller power of expression that can result from bringing these two languages together.

A Lifeline, Not Just a Hook

It is important to recognize that art can be much more than a hook used to capture a student's interest or to provide a transient reward for cooperating with an otherwise unappealing lesson. Over the past two decades of work in the trenches, I have met hundreds of students of all ages, students who, for one reason or another, struggled with reading and writing. Many of these students had also become discouraged learners and chose to distance themselves from school's daily challenges and frustrations. This is true not only for those first learning how to read and write but also for older students as well. Mark comes to mind:

Mark was a discouraged sixth grader who refused to participate in just about every classroom activity. With his own unique set of learning and organizational challenges, he found completing any task difficult. On the rare occasion that he did complete an activity, he usually lost his work soon thereafter. His basic attitude about schoolwork was, "Why bother?"

That was until he was enticed into constructing a story by a purple marbleized paper he had created, in which he spotted a gigantic sea monster. With his very own handmade marbleized paper in hand and his imagination sparked by his sea monster sighting, Mark dove into constructing his collage story with vigor. Though his impulsive nature continued to challenge him, with some gentle guidance he persevered and managed to steer himself through crafting an entire story sequence of collage images that told his tale. The sequence of pictures also helped Mark to anchor his story and organize his thoughts on paper once he began to write. In his chicken-scratch handwriting, he wrote fervently, his sense of ownership and engagement apparent. When Mark completed his story (which he managed not to lose), his sense of pride and accomplishment was clear.

At the end of the project, Mark's teacher asked her students to write down their reflections about the art-based writing process they had just experienced. Mark, who rarely if ever responded to such requests, scratched out the following two sentences: "It influenced me to write because it is cool." and "If you don't have an idea, pictures will give you a good idea." (See Figure 2.2.) As the students discussed their reflections in class, Jamie, one of Mark's classmates, read her reflection, "It was easier to think of ideas for stories because somehow the pictures set your imagination working overtime."

While initially this art-based approach to writing clearly provided the necessary hook to engage Mark, it offered much more. It gave him concrete, hands-on tools for developing, expressing, and recording his ideas. Engagement alone should not be and cannot be the only goal. As educators, we must find ways to truly support our low-performing

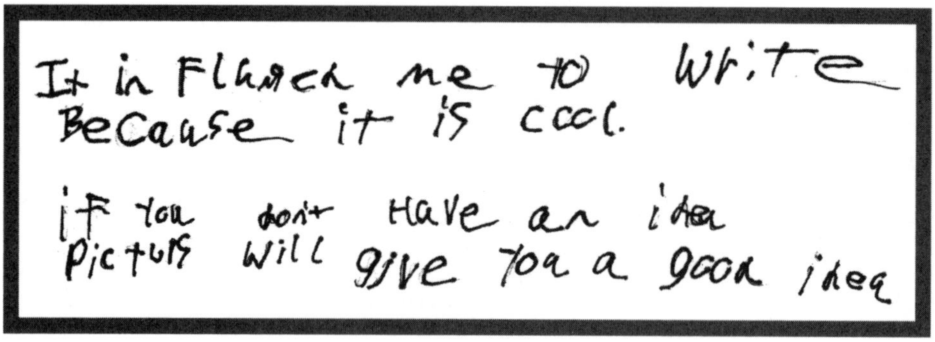

It in Flhach me to write
Because it is cool.

if you don't Have an idea
picturs will give you a good idea

Figure 2.2.   Mark's handwritten reflection.

students both emotionally and academically. How do we help reluctant or discouraged learners improve their skills?

Not, I should hope, by forcing them to confront their weaknesses day in and day out and insisting they spend hour after hour in what appears to them—and therefore *is*—pointless drudgery. We must remember that many of our low-performing students do indeed have strengths, often as visual, tactual, or kinesthetic learners, or some combination thereof. Attempting to force such students to learn via verbal instructions and verbal exercises alone makes no sense. They have already proven to us time and again that these methods do not work for them. As an educational system, are we the ones slow to learn?

Educators face a challenge: beyond adjusting our teaching to meet the needs of all students, we must invite all our students into a classroom community that honors, respects, and employs their unique gifts and talents. We must offer them learning experiences that promise not only to be fun *for them* but also allow them to use their strengths to develop new skills in their areas of relative weakness. We must attempt to level the playing field by giving all students opportunities to shine.

The approach I have developed clearly moves in this direction. Before long, your top students may be asking your (formerly) "low-performing students" for help drawing, thus giving those students an opportunity to share their talents with their peers. You may also discover that those very same students, when given tools aligned with their strengths, display surprising levels of creativity and success—even in their writing. When your low-performing students are academically or behaviorally challenged, enticing them into engagement through offering them opportunities to use their strengths (and coincidently engaging them in activities they enjoy) is likely to profoundly alter the dynamics within your classroom. Offer students a variety of simple yet rich art processes and a progression of literature-based mini-lessons, invite them into the inner circle of artists and writers, and you will witness new levels of engagement and enthusiasm for learning. As Geoffrey and Renate Nummela Caine remind us: when motivation is high, so is learning.

Highlights of the Research

It is true that much of the research on the impact of the arts on student achievement has failed to establish a significant causal link between participation in the arts and increased academic achievement (Deasey, 2002; Eisner, 1998; Winner and Cooper, 2000). Nonetheless, the particular art-infused approach to literacy learning I describe here has been able to establish strong causal links to writing achievement—as well as to reading.

Two quantitative studies documented the performance of students participating in Artists/Writers Workshop as compared to demographically matched groups who did not participate, one in 1991–1993 and the other in 1997–1998. These two studies tracked numerous specific gains in writing performance and use of art as a language among students considered at risk at the beginning of the study as well as those who were not considered to be at risk. Both groups far outpaced demographically matched students in the comparison group. In addition, since the second study expanded on the research model used in the first, it was possible to establish that more is better—the nine-month process tracked in the second study produced even greater gains than the three-month process tracked in the first. The results of these studies are included in Appendix A, along with reading and writing standardized test score data that grew out of a subsequent school-wide adoption. The test score results of Title I and Special Education students over time are most impressive—the sort of thing every school would wish to achieve in response to the mandates of No Child Left Behind.

part two

The Workshop Process

3 Reading

Study of Quality Picture Books

Oh, my! This is my first time to make book.
You know, Teacher, I love my book.
I used to hate reading. Now I love to read, Teacher.

—Angeline, Grade 3

Riding in a car, a passenger tends to sit back and enjoy the scenery as it streams past. A driver is much more observant. Being responsible for the journey, the driver must notice important landmarks that will be helpful in learning the way. A passenger who is about to take over the driving is also apt to pay more attention to the route.

Likewise, when students see themselves as artists and writers—when their teacher gives them the task of creating their own quality picture books—they in effect move from the passenger's seat to the driver's seat. They become active participants in the literary process rather than passive observers of someone else's story. They notice important landmarks (literary elements), and they begin to create their own road maps for creating quality art and writing. In the process, en route, they become stronger readers as they focus their efforts on the work of a writer (which involves learning to read like a writer as well as reading and rereading their own written text). I witness this phenomenon over and over again, year after year. The following story offers one example:

Peter was repeating first grade the year I worked with him. Having shown little interest in learning how to read or write, Peter found his pathway into story through constructing collage image after collage image. He built his story with the same ease with which he built forts out of sticks at the edge of the schoolyard. Once he finished his sequence of images, he was eager to share his story with his classmates. He proceeded to read his pictures as if he were reading a book.

Peter then wanted to record the words to his story. He knew he would have to do so in order to get his book published along with his classmates. He did so using rudimentary invented spelling. As he finished writing each page, he then had to read it over to make sure it made sense. Sounding out the words did not come easily to Peter, even in his own invented spelling, but he stuck with it, reading and rereading his words before writing each new page. Once Peter finished writing his story, it was typed up in standard spelling and published with his collage images in the form of a spiral-bound book.

Peter was then eager to learn how to read the typed version of the story he had so carefully crafted so he could share his book with his classmates. Although that was even more difficult for him, he was willing to put in the extra effort because he was excited about the story he had constructed with his very own hands. To this day, I recall the pride on Peter's face as he read his professional-looking published collage story to his classmates for the first time. It was the very first book Peter had ever read cover to cover.

Using Picture Books as Mentor Texts

Students participating in Artists/Writers Workshop study illustrations as well as text from an insider's perspective. As they prepare to craft their own quality picture books, students learn how to see like an artist and how to read like a writer. Interestingly, the former helps them make progress with the latter.

Focusing on the Illustrations: Reading the Pictures

When I introduce the distinct roles that pictures and words play within a picture book, I find it helpful to separate the two languages. I begin by asking students, "What is the job of the pictures in a picture book?" Usually at least a few students will tell me that the pictures in a picture book tell the story. I then invite the whole class to be the judges, to determine if the pictures in the book I am about to share do tell the story. I select a picture book that I think will provide a strong model, one in which the pictures really do tell the story and one that is unfamiliar to my students. Then I lead the class in the whole-group task of reading the pictures, page by page, as I hide the text. I even hide the title when I show students the cover, thus removing all information provided by the language of words. I ask the class to guess what the story is about by looking at the cover picture. No matter what students tell me, I ask them, "How do you know that?" Having to answer this question repeatedly builds their understanding of the connection between the visual information and the meaning they glean.

Isolating the pictures from the text makes it easier to consider the job of the pictures. As I show students each page of the story (while hiding the text), I ask the same simple question: "What does this picture tell about?" In the absence of supporting text, students begin to read each picture with much more attention to detail than they otherwise might give it. Each time a student offers a piece of information, I ask, "How do you know that?" This dual questioning process continues page by page until the class has examined each picture for meaning.

As students develop their visual literacy, they begin to understand that every visual choice the artist has made, every detail regarding subject and color and composition, conveys information that informs the reader. This attention to visual details provides an important foundation for the students' understanding of the precise role of the artist, which will be critical as they take on the task of creating their own picture books.

After walking students through the reading of pictures in a picture book page by page, I ask another key question: "Do you think the pictures in this picture book do a good job of telling the story?" If I have chosen a picture book with well-crafted and detailed images, the students will generally agree that the pictures do a good job telling the story. When

I ask them what aspect of the pictures is most important in telling the story, they will often recognize that it is the attention to detail that helps tell the story. This prepares students for creating their own picture story as they transfer this understanding to the creation of their own quality picture books. This Literature Share/Discussion primes their minds for appreciating the importance of detail in other aspects of their work.

Considering the Job of the Words

Next (on either the same or a different day), I say to students, "We all agreed that the job of the pictures in a picture book is to tell the story. So what do you think the job of the words is?" Most students will tell me that the words also tell the story. To help them understand how the job of the words differs from the job of the pictures, I read students the very same picture book. This time I read the story while showing the pictures, allowing the class to experience the marriage of text and image. (As I read, I am careful to hold the book in such a way that students can see the pictures as I read the words.) To call attention to how the words serve a function beyond the pictures in telling the story, for each page I ask, "What did you discover from the words that you had not known from reading the picture?"

When we finish reading the story, I say to students, "You told me that the pictures did a good job telling the story, so what is the job of the words?" Students will often tell me that the words have provided information that the pictures alone do not (and cannot) convey. Students observe that words can expand upon or enhance the meaning of the pictures in a variety of ways:

- ✦ Providing background information (something that happened in the past)
- ✦ Locating the story in a specific time or place
- ✦ Enhancing the mood
- ✦ Drawing the reader's eye to certain aspects of the picture that might otherwise have gone unnoticed
- ✦ Introducing other senses such as sound, smell, or touch
- ✦ Telling the reader how to interpret the picture

Students come to recognize that while pictures can tell a story, words can move the reader beyond what the language of pictures alone can convey, providing more details and more specific information. The key point is that *together the words and pictures tell the whole story.* It is not uncommon to hear even young students remark that the words made the picture "come alive!" To the driver's eye—the participatory eye of a student crafter of picture books—this makes the words vastly more interesting as a topic of study, particularly to those captivated by the picture-making and storytelling process.

Beyond Decorative Detail

Despite the countless examples of outstanding picture books that contain exceptional artwork and in which the pictures are clearly as important as the words, those pictures tend to be seen as secondary—as mere illustrations that accompany the text. This notion is reinforced by the picture book publishing process itself, for unless a picture book is written and illustrated by the same person, the text is typically written first and then the publisher assigns a "proven illustrator" to the project, someone who will then create illustrations to accompany the text. Driven by the belief that well-known illustrators boost the market value of picture books, the book-creation process has indeed become text-driven. Of course, this is not the only reason. Another factor that plays heavily into this reality is that we are schooled to believe that stories are created and driven by text.

It is interesting to note, however, that some picture books created by a sole author–illustrator (as would be the case with students in the classroom) did start with the pictures (*Water Dance* by Thomas Locker (1997), for instance). Author and illustrator Eric Carle (1993) acknowledges his enjoyment of the option to move back and forth between words and pictures.

In fact, whether we acknowledge it or not, the picturing process is an integral part of writing or even telling a story. Phrases such as *reading a story* or *telling a story* emphasize the traditional verbal view of story as something that relies upon words. Nonetheless, what a writer or story-teller does when composing a compelling tale or telling a captivating story is to *paint pictures with words*. These "mental pictures" are at the root of comprehension, whether the audience is listening to the story or reading it. Nanci Bell (1991) notes how intricately connected reading comprehension is to the ability to *visualize* what is being read. Whether the words are written on paper or spoken aloud, understanding what is being conveyed by these words naturally entails envisioning what the words say. Without this innate picturing process, verbal communication (spoken or written) would be impossible.

By studying the role of pictures within picture books, students learn a great deal about both the language of pictures and the language of words. They open their eyes to phenomena otherwise likely to go unnoticed. As they study each element of a story from an insider's perspective, using both the more concrete, easily accessible language of pictures and the more abstract language of words, they are driven by their natural love of story, the engagement offered by the picture-making process, and their excitement over the possibility of words making their own pictures "come alive." In the process of preparing to create and then creating their own quality picture books, they become more adept painters of pictures (actual and mental) and more perceptive interpreters of visual and written language; they become *readers*.

Picture Books for Older Students

Sometimes teachers question the practice of using picture books with older students. They are concerned that older students will view picture books as "babyish." In *Craft Lessons*, Ralph Fletcher and JoAnn Portalupi (1998) recommend using quality picture books when teaching writing to upper grade students, even high school students. Because picture books are so succinct, they can be easily read, reread, and analyzed during a class period. And reading a quality picture book, itself a work of art, can be rewarding to study for people of any age.

Although picture books can be a wonderful teaching tool for students of any age, they do need to be matched to the interests and sophistication of the audience. When I read picture books to older students, I am careful in my choice of books, steering away from picture books that are clearly cute and designed for very young children. *Owl Moon*, written by Jane Yolen and illustrated by John Schoenherr, is a favorite of mine to share with students of all ages. (In Chapter Eight, I discuss details of using *Owl Moon* in the classroom.) For students whose preferred medium isn't words, a book like this can provide a critical bridge into literacy learning—the pictures serve to draw the students in and tell enough of the story so that, when combined with the words, they create that critical element of sheer engagement that whets students' interest and drives their desire to learn.

Why Improvement in Reading?

The process described in this book was developed for the purpose of improving students' writing skills, which makes the impressive reading results documented by standardized test score data, particularly for Title I and Special Education students (described in Appendix A), especially interesting. Given that reading instruction was not part of the intervention and no new reading interventions were introduced during the years that standardized test score data was collected, it is natural to wonder why this approach to writing has such a positive impact on reading achievement, particularly for those who struggle with reading.

To begin, once again it is necessary to acknowledge the dynamic interplay of visual and verbal modalities throughout the process. Keep in mind that many low-performing students exhibit strengths as visual, tactual, and kinesthetic learners and seem to thrive when given the opportunity to use these modalities. Embedded in this art-based approach to writing exist several recognized best practices from the field of literacy learning: daily read-alouds of quality picture books, the regular use of picture books as mentor texts (for the study of both the language of pictures and the language of words), attention to reading the details in illustrations through "book walks" (a comprehension strategy), the purposeful reading of nonfiction text and illustrations to gather information relevant to inquiry-based integrated curriculum writing projects, the reading that naturally occurs during the writing process as students read and reread their own work during drafting and revision,

the reading and rereading of students' own published books as they prepare for their Artists/Writers Celebrations, and finally the reading of
each other's published books, which are kept in the classroom library.

Furthermore, within Artists/Writers Workshop, students typically
delight in learning how "silver dollar words" (described in Chapter
Five) can paint pictures in the reader's mind. They listen purposefully
to text to determine if the author's words paint pictures in their minds;
they listen to their own and each other's writing to determine whether
those words paint pictures. This ability to visualize, to see a "movie in
one's mind" as one reads or is read to, is critical to successful reading
comprehension (Bell, 1991). Seeing if words create mental pictures is a
common practice within this visual approach to literacy learning. This
was made clear by six-year old Steven at the end of his first-grade year
when his teacher Sue Rafferty asked her first graders to reflect on what
they learned in Artists/Writers Workshop. Steven wrote:

> In Artists/Writers Workshop, I love my art very much. I did
> good pictures on all of my art and very nice words. I use silver
> dollar words. I get published books. I write stories that paint
> pictures in Mrs. Rafferty's mind.

As students stretch to include words that paint pictures in their own
writing, they find themselves writing with increased descriptive language
("silver dollar words,"). While the use of invented spelling allows even
emergent writers to include challenging descriptive language in their writing at will, once these words are typed using standard spelling and appear
in their published pieces, students (like Peter) find themselves faced with
the challenge of having to stretch their decoding skills to read their own
writing. Eager to read their very own handcrafted published pieces out
loud to their friends and family, students are highly motivated to tackle
sounding out these challenging words. I have had first-grade teachers initially express concern that their students had trouble reading their newly
published book and the same teachers later express amazement at the
words their emergent readers learned how to sound out.

Finally, and perhaps most interestingly, the very act of seeing themselves as artists and crafters of picture books naturally results in students' viewing the world through the eyes of an artist. They develop

a heightened sense of visual interest, awareness, and purpose. As they watch the sky change from dawn to sunrise or from sunset to twilight, they may wonder what color paint they would use to capture those colors on paper. They may also take mental snapshots of these beautiful skies in order to recreate them later as they paint. They may look intently at the structure, color, and texture of trees. As a result of viewbving themselves as crafters of picture books, students engage regularly in intentional observation of the world around them and then retain, recall, and recreate their stored mental images on paper (in pictures and in words) as they live the life of an artist and writer. This too serves to strengthen their ability to visualize, to produce visual representations, and to paint pictures with words as they craft their own literary masterpieces. This heightened ability to visualize supports them not only as artists but also as writers and as readers.

All these very natural and almost seamlessly intertwined activities serve not only to strengthen students' skills as artists, as writers, and as readers, but also to capture their interest and motivate them to excel. Fourth-grade teacher Violy Bertrain, from the island of Saipan, shares this story with amusement: "My students, they didn't want to stop! At recess they say, 'Ma'am, can we stay inside' I say, 'Why?' They say, 'We want to work on our stories!' At lunch, this happened too. . . . In the morning, they would come into school and say, 'Ma'am, can we work on our stories now?' They didn't want to do anything else!" A veteran teacher, Violy had never seen anything motivate her students in quite this way.

While motivation and engagement are high among students of all backgrounds and levels of verbal ability as they create their own quality picture books, the success and pride experienced by those at risk (who are generally not successful in the reading and writing arena) are critical to their continued growth in literacy. Angeline, a third-grade student and English language learner from Saipan, confessed, "I even hated to read before." With pride, she added, "Now I love reading and making stories!" Angeline's teacher, Luz Buccat, recalls, "How I wish you could have seen my Angeline when I gave her back her published book. She takes it in her arms like this and embraces it. 'Oh, my!' she says. 'This is my first time to make book. You know, Teacher, I love my book. I used to hate reading. Now I love to read, Teacher." Luz adds with great pride, " Now my Angeline is even reading chapter books."

Luz pulls out a letter she received from one of her third-grade students at the end of the year.

Dear Mrs. Buccat,

Last September, how come you taught us how to make book? We never did this in our life! Image-Making is so much fun and thank you for teaching us how to make book. I feel great.

Your student,
Steven

Luz continues,

But it is not just my Angeline and Steven. Image-Making has affected all my students. In the beginning, they didn't bother much to read. It was hard for them to pick up a book to read. They never did this. Now they say, "Oh, Teacher, I like to read that [Image-Making] book again!" They want to read each other's books! They have started to love to read!

And before their writing was flat. No salt and pepper. Now they write with description. They even ask, "Teacher, can we make another book?" I have never seen such a thing.

Teachers and administrators will be interested to know that students' success and growing self-efficacy is apparent not only in their behavior and attitude but also in their impressive standardized test scores in both writing *and* reading. (See Appendix A.) My hope is that someday, within the field of education, we will universally recognize the complex, intricate, and dynamic relationship between picture-making, writing, and reading and ultimately come to redefine the 3 R's as reading, writing, and art.

4　Art

Thinking in Pictures

I always make my pictures first because then
I can get looks at them to help me with my describing words.
If I wrote my words first, I wouldn't be able to see
my describing words in my pictures.

—Hannah, Grade 3

After nearly two decades exploring art and writing in the classroom with students grades K–8, I have come to believe that students make greater gains as writers if teachers recognize and honor the tremendous thinking that occurs during the making of art. Indeed, the more attention teachers and students give to creating pictures, the greater the thinking—with the most comprehensive thinking occurring when students actually draft their ideas fully in pictures before beginning to write. I also have come to believe that the richer the art materials used, the richer the visual representations that result, and the richer the thought that accompanies the picture-making experience. Furthermore, the richer and more thoughtful the picture-making experience, the richer (in detail and description) the writing that grows from that experience. Simply put, if we want students to paint detailed pictures with their words, we need to teach them how to think in detail. This is accomplished (at least at first) by creating detailed images using quality art materials. It is part of the "learning to visualize" process so vital to creating strong readers and writers.

Lost in the Traditional Verbal Shuffle

As a visual and kinesthetic learner myself, I can tell you right now, words are not a preferred medium for thinking for most visual, tactual, or kinesthetic learners. Dr. Sue Teele's inventory of learning strengths (Figure 1.1 and Table 1.1 in Chapter One) reminds us that many students' strengths lie in areas other than the verbal or written arena (Brudnak, 1995). What few educators realize is that if only we could rid ourselves of the pervasive verbal bias within our educational system, monumental shifts would occur in our teaching practices and in our students' learning. For the sake of argument, set aside the idea that pictures have little or no role to play in writing instruction. With fresh eyes observing the behaviors and strengths of low-performing students, I think it would become obvious that schools have been overlooking a critical pathway into literacy learning for our visual and kinesthetic learners: Art.

Although this point of view is contrary to the way most teachers have been taught to teach writing, and seemingly counterintuitive (particularly to verbally oriented or verbally trained educators), my own years of inquiry into the rich relationship between pictures and words have led me to believe that encouraging students to make their pictures first, *before they write,* can often be critical to their success; it is as important as immersing students in quality literature. And I am not talking about merely creating "rehearsal drawings," a practice allowed emergent writers in writing process classrooms. One critical shift that I have made beyond the "rehearsal drawings" concept is not only to encourage students to make their pictures first, before they write, but also to emphasize the fact that in these pictures, students are "creating art"—not merely making perfunctory pencil sketches.

Art Enhances Thought: Materials Matter

For the discouraged learner, the reluctant writer, or even those uncomfortable "doing art," the materials can make all the difference. When teachers try to limit effort in the name of convenience by offering students markers, crayons, or colored pencils to develop pictures for their stories, they overlook two important facts: the medium itself can serve to hook reluctant learners, and it will determine the kinds of thinking available to students. Many teachers do not realize the profound impact both of these have on story development and the use of descriptive language. Quality art materials, and the enriched art experiences that result, serve many purposes:

+ They entice students (reluctant or not) into engaging in the rehearsal, drafting, and revision experience without even realizing it.

+ They extend students' thinking and the development of their ideas simply through engaging them in the art process.

+ They encourage students' use of descriptive language.

+ They enhance students' self-esteem by making it relatively easy to produce a quality product.

The kinds of art materials typically available in the classroom (colored markers, colored pencils, and crayons) pale in comparison to other art media, not only in terms of their ability to lure budding young artists and writers into the writing process (particularly those who are reluctant to express themselves), but also in their ability to generate ideas and descriptive language. While some classroom teachers may be reluctant to "get out the paints," I can assure those committed to cultivating enthusiastic and skillful writers that it is worthwhile to offer a richer selection of art materials and processes than the typical classroom fare, along with some simple guidelines. If you are among the teachers who immediately think, "But I don't know how to do that," I hope that the sample mini-lessons and DVD companion will provide enough guidance to enable you and your students to experiment with the process.

Media

I have found two types of art medium particularly suited to the in-class construction of picture books: crayon resist painting and collage created out of hand-painted textured papers made by the students. Both techniques offer a depth of color and texture, with opportunities for "happy accidents" that make for astonishingly beautiful and surprising results. Self-proclaimed non-artists and non-writers of any age often find themselves looking at the results and, like David, saying, "I didn't know I could do that good."

Over my many years of fascination and continued exploration utilizing these two art processes in the classroom, I have developed two fully fleshed-out models: Picturing Writing: Fostering Literacy Through Art, which uses crayon resist, and Image-Making Within The Writing Process, which uses collage made from hand-painted textured papers. (See the color plate section for examples of each process.) These models extend far beyond the use of a particular art technique or medium, offering a comprehensive and systematic art-based approach to literacy learning. While these two models are not the focus of this book, the thinking behind their development is central to my evolving understanding of literacy learning. The research results presented in Appendix A document the impact specifically of Picturing Writing and Image-Making on students' reading, writing, and art skills. More information about both these models is available at www.picturingwriting.org.

Crayon Resist

Crayon resist (creating a crayon drawing and then painting over it with a watercolor wash) offers students a simple, appealing art process for developing and expressing their ideas. It offers teachers a simple and easy-to-manage classroom art technique, making it a good way to enter the Artists/Writers Workshop process.

I am particularly partial to this technique because most children are already familiar with and comfortable using crayons. Crayon is fairly easy to control and can be used to create representational images. Meanwhile, watercolor is harder to control but offers more opportunities for nuances in shading and color. When a watercolor wash is applied over a crayon drawing, the wax of the crayon resists the paint (thus, crayon resist), and the effect is quite pleasing. The watercolor is immediately absorbed into the areas of the paper that have not been colored with crayon, creating a rich nuanced effect not achievable with crayon alone, or with color pencils or markers (the typical classroom fare). (See Color Plate E.) For more detailed information on the crayon resist process, see the mini-lesson "Painting Sunset—Introducing Crayon Resist" in Chapter Nine and watch the DVD chapter, "Complete Crayon Resist Lesson."

Unlike tempera or other opaque paint, watercolor will create a luscious translucent quality that enhances any picture and makes it more likely to provoke imaginative thought and language.

During one of her very first crayon resist painting sessions, six-year-old Melanie created a picture of a wintry twilight using white crayon to make snow and painting a violet watercolor wash across the sky. When her painting was placed in the Artists Frame during the Group Share, Melanie eagerly hopped up into the Artists Chair. Given the chance to look at her painting more carefully—with an artist's eye, she spotted a faint white dot in her violet sky, which had occurred accidentally during the painting process. When she was asked to tell about her painting, she noticed the dim white marking for the very first time. Excited, she jumped out of the Artists Chair and made her way to the Artists Frame where she pointed to the barely perceptible tiny white spot on her painting. She proudly announced to her classmates that it was the very first star of the night. Later, when it came time to write about her painting, Melanie remembered her discovery and in invented spelling, wrote: "It is twilight. The sun has gone to bed. The first star is peeking out of the violet sky."

The naturally occurring nuances created during the watercolor painting process often make it possible for artists to discover details beyond what they originally intended. From reading the pictures for details to orally rehearsing what you see in your picture, to including those details in written descriptions is a fairly simple matter, even for the youngest of writers. Brainstorming sheets (discussed in Chapter Five), which help students read their pictures for information, also support this process.

Several texturing techniques can be added to the crayon resist process to encourage the inclusion of more detail. Tissue clouds (modeled on the DVD), scratch technique (using a toothpick or wooden paint brush handle to make ripples in water, tree bark, wind, rain, animal fur), white tempera splattered, sponged, or dabbed to make snow or foam on water, and salt sprinkled on wet watercolor to create a glistening effect can all greatly enhance the kinds of thinking and descriptive language available to young artists and writers, without adding much difficulty to the classroom crayon resist process. In my experience, the added detail and texture often translate directly into imaginative thought and rich language. (See Color Plates F, G, and H.)

While these simple techniques delight students of all ages, I recommend introducing only the most basic tissue clouds (modeled on the DVD) early in the process. Allow your students to master the basics, beginning simply and then later introducing the other supplemental techniques.

First grader Devin's shark painting (Color Plate G) was created using a combination of crayon resist and white tempera sponging. To it, he created this haiku-like poem:

> *Big black shark*
> *Swimming in stormy waters.*
> *Likes foamy waves!*

Collage Made with Hand-Painted Textured Papers

When I first began to investigate the impact of art-based writing in the classroom in the fall of 1990, Eric Carle had been chosen as the author/ illustrator for the month of September. His bright, bold collage images delighted the first- and second-grade students I was working with and inspired my early explorations using collage made from hand-painted textured papers. I was immediately impressed by the benefit of having students create their own hand-painted papers rather than creating collage using ready-made materials. Students were instantly drawn into the process by their natural curiosity and fascination with the varied effects that can be created by applying paint to paper using very simple art techniques.

The paper-texturing techniques were all designed for immediate success even for those with little or no art background. Students created portfolios of fascinating abstract designs by floating pigments on water to produce marbleized paper; experimenting with watercolor on wet paper and watercolor with salt; creating plastic wrap prints; splattering paint on wet and on dry paper; and dabbing paint onto paper with sponges, to name just a few of the possibilities. I soon found that students' engagement in the paper-texturing process led to a sense of ownership and pride not only over the colorful and varied papers they created but also over the stories that grew out of these hand-painted papers. This experience has been repeated by every group I have witnessed from ages five to adult—except for one, described later in this chapter. Looking at their individual portfolios of hand-painted textured papers, students invariably find their creative juices began to flow. The resulting tales are often as rich and surprising as the art processes that sparked them.

While one student discovered a churning ocean in a bubble painting, which inspired a story about a ship that got lost at sea in a storm, another discovered long wispy feathers in her green marbleized papers, which sparked a story about a peacock. A third discovered an "Ice Crackler" in his plastic wrap print—a fantastic creature that made ice in its belly and spit it out through its enormous jaws. Each of these story ideas grew directly out of images the students discovered in their portfolios of hand-painted papers. The original Image-Making process actually evolved out of this ability of hand-painted textured papers to inspire imaginative "discovered stories" (Olshansky, 1998). Such was the case with Amanda, a fifth-grader whose portfolio of beautiful papers inspired a story about a young girl who was invited by the sun to paint sunrise and sunset in the sky each day (see Figure 4.1).

Figure 4.1.   Cover of Amanda's collage story

On the back cover of her published book, *Sarena and the Beautiful Skies* (1995), Amanda describes her experience with the process:

> I got the idea for this book from one of my Plexiglas prints. It reminded me of a sunset. Once I had my basic idea, then page by page, I made my collage pictures. Making collages gave me more ideas for my story. Then I just looked at each of my pictures and wrote what came to mind. As I kept writing, the words just flowed together to make unique descriptions. I think this way of writing is much more fun. It made me think more creatively.

Color Plate I shows one of Amanda's collages and an example of the kinds of language that "just flowed together" to make Amanda's unique descriptions.

Supporting Continued Story Line Development

In addition to students' discovering imaginative stories hidden in their portfolios of hand-painted paper, I have also observed how these textured papers have supported the continued development of a story line as the students literally construct their stories. Figure 4.2 displays the cover of one such story.

Picture nine-year-old Kelsea in the midst of fashioning a collage story about a fishing trip. The inspiration is a blue marbleized paper that reminds her of water and the lake where she and her dad often fish.

The story takes an imaginative twist as Kelsea creates her next collage in which she falls asleep and dreams that she and her friend turn into "two wiggly worms." She constructs a series of imaginative collages that take her on a harrowing adventure in which her dad puts her on a fishing hook and casts her out into the lake. (See Color Plate J.) Notice her dramatic use of changes in perspective as she takes us on her journey. From a long distance picture, above the water, her next collage image takes us into the water and down to the bottom of the lake. It also draws us in closer so we can see what is about to become of the poor worm.

Figure 4.2.   Kelsea's cover.

Just as a large sunset-colored salmon comes along ready to devour her whole, Kelsea is not sure what will happen next. (See Color Plate K.) With her hand-painted papers spread out around her on the floor, her eyes land on a purple and magenta marbleized paper she forgot to comb. It reminds her of the inside of a fish. She knows exactly what will happen next! She decides to use the paper whole, affixing to it two eyes, a teeth-lined mouth, and a portion of a worm (her friend) half-way into the mouth. She adds a second blue worm (representing her), already inside the fish, which has squirmed over to the eye to look out. To this dramatic close-up, Kelsea writes:

> Inside the sunset salmon, she felt sick. She wondered if she would ever get out. She squirmed over to the eye and peeked out as if it were a window. She looked for her friend, but her friend was nowhere to be seen. All she could see was the sandy floor and some seaweed swaying back and forth. She felt quite frightened. (See Color Plate L).

As Kelsea constructs her story, her hand-painted papers provide inspiration and unusual perspectives (I mean this literally) that she might otherwise never have considered. For her final collage, she discovers a deep blue watercolor and salt painting that reminds her of a night sky. In this next collage, she cleverly and dramatically pulls us away from the intensity of being trapped inside the fish and once again offers us the big-picture, long-distance view shown in Figure 4.3. She ends the story neatly:

> All of a sudden, the girl woke up. She found herself back in her boat staring up at the glistening stars. She sat up and leaned over the side of the boat. Sunset salmon were jumping all around! The young girl smiled to herself.

If Kelsea had been drafting her story in words first or had been creating "rehearsal drawings" using the typical crayons, colored markers,

Figure 4.3.   The very last picture in Kelsea's book.

or colored pencils, her imaginative story idea would never have occurred to her, nor would it have taken such surprising and imaginative twists. Her hand-painted textured papers were indeed instrumental not only in launching her story but also in its evolving plot development. I am convinced that Kelsea's story *Sunset Dream* (1998) never would have been created had it not been for the imaginative workings of her mind as she interacted with her hand-painted papers. Nor would she have arrived at such dramatic and effective uses of changes in perspective had she been asked to write first or had been given the standard classroom fare for making pictures.

Use Quality Materials

The importance of using quality art materials was reinforced when I was called into a school on an "emergency consultation." The entire school of nearly six hundred students had made hand-painted textured papers as they eagerly launched an Image-Making project. It had been a huge school-wide undertaking that occurred with the help of many parent-volunteers. Students traveled from classroom to classroom through grade level wings creating a total of fifteen thousand hand-painted textured papers. It was an all-day event and a huge school-community effort. After all the hand-painted papers had dried, classroom teachers organized each student's work into individual portfolios and then invited students to look through their hand-painted papers to discover the story hidden within their individual portfolios. It was here that the process began to break down. Rather than coming up with a wide range of imaginative ideas, all the students could see was gray clouds and rain—dull, gray rain and puddles.

The school asked me to determine what went wrong and how to get the project back on track. When I saw the students' portfolios, I knew immediately what the problem was. In an effort to economize, the organizers had purchased the most inexpensive watercolors and paintbrushes they could find. Unfortunately, this resulted in thousands of hand-painted papers that were mainly tinted shades of gray. The papers appeared washed out. The students' story ideas were as dull as the papers.

My advice to the principal was hard to swallow: either organize another round of paper painting/texturing using quality watercolors or trash the entire project. Fortunately for the students, the principal decided on the former. The lesson learned was a costly one: use art materials that support the process. Reasonably priced quality art materials will, in the end, better serve both you and your students. (For more information about materials, visit www.picturingwriting.org/artsupplies.html.)

Quality Materials Inspire Rich Language

Another reminder about the importance of the quality of the art materials occurred when I was invited into a second-grade classroom to view students' completed collage books. The class had been so enthusiastic about creating their first stories made from their own hand-painted textured papers that the students asked their teacher if they could make a second story. Delighted by their enthusiasm, she did not hesitate to say yes. As her students' portfolios of hand-painted textured papers grew thin and the community box of shared papers quickly emptied, this well-intentioned teacher went to her supply closet and pulled out reams of colored construction paper that she then placed in the community box. While the second generation of students' books began with collages made from the students' hand-painted papers, by the middle of these books their supply of papers had dwindled. The collages in the middle of their stories consisted of a mix of hand-painted papers and construction paper. The final pages of the students' stories consisted of collage made entirely out of construction paper.

As I read through these stories, I was struck by the progression of images and text from beginning to end. Not only were the images on the final pages (those made entirely from construction paper) much less vibrant and appealing, but the text followed the same pattern. The first pages, written to the collages made from hand-painted papers, contained rich descriptive language. The middle pages (a mix of hand-painted papers and construction paper) contained significantly less descriptive language. The language that accompanied the final collage images (those fashioned entirely from construction paper) was as flat as the construction paper itself. The only conclusion I could draw was that materials matter; these students had clearly demonstrated their ability to use rich verbal imagery, but as the surfaces they worked with lost a richness of color, variety, and texture, their descriptive language became as flat as the construction paper images they had fashioned.

Everyone Is an Artist

One of the underlying assumptions of Artists/Writers Workshop is that everyone is an artist. *I Am an Artist* by Pat Lowery Collins makes this point clearly, which is why I like to use that book to introduce Artists/ Writers Workshop (see Chapter Nine). If you find your enthusiasm beginning to wane at the thought of having to model making a picture in front of the class, let me remind you of a few things:

+ Nearly every picture you make, your students will think is marvelous (young students can provide a particularly appreciative audience).

+ Should your older students see and listen to you struggle, they are apt to be sympathetic and offer you some useful tips.

+ A few simple artist tips (and the demonstration lessons on the DVD) can boost your understanding of how to create an effective picture easily and how to teach this to your students.

+ Practice will create more comfort with the materials and the process.

If you see yourself as a reluctant artist, try explaining to your class that you are a learner and you will be joining your students in this journey of discovery. I think you will find that your students will be very supportive and appreciative of your sharing your personal learning experiences alongside them. Together with your students, you will form a classroom community of learners exploring and discovering together. (You could also engage the help of your school's art specialist, if he or she is willing.)

It is important to remember that, like writing, art is a *process*. In much the same way that no one expects students to be expert writers without practice or instruction, we shouldn't expect that of student artists—or of ourselves. Be honest with your students about how you feel about doing art and show them that your desire to learn overrides your trepidation.

Isn't that modeling exactly what you expect of your students? Also keep in mind that the class art and writing pieces, co-created by you and your students, will provide opportunities to discuss and model revision of both pictures and words. The work need not be perfect from the start. You are modeling a *process!*

When you model creating a piece of art, talk through your intentions with your students. Once you finish, reflect on what parts of your picture you are content with and what parts you might like to revise. Solicit suggestions for revision. This will set the stage not only for students to learn how to offer and receive suggestions but also for students to engage in meaningful revision practices themselves (of both pictures and words).

It is my hope that by reading this book, studying the work of professional illustrators, and viewing the companion DVD, you will gain enough confidence to take that initial leap of faith. If you still feel you would benefit from hands-on instruction, seek out one of my many experiential teacher-training workshops! (To find out more, visit www .picturingwriting.org.)

Choosing a Medium

As processes, crayon resist and collage made from hand-painted textured papers offer opportunities for very different kinds of art-making as well as different kinds of thinking.

Crayon resist is a simpler process for teachers as well as for students, and it offers a more immediate product (because it doesn't involve first creating a portfolio of papers to use in constructing collage images). Once a student becomes adept at crayon resist and the array of supplemental texturing techniques possible, the process can equal the use of textured papers in its ability to elicit descriptive language. Crayon resist is a great place to begin exploring Artists/Writers Workshop. The Picturing Writing process (which is based in crayon resist) also offers a systematic progression of art-and-literature-based mini-lessons that teach basic skills in a simple, easy-to-grasp manner. It is with this process that I recommend students and teachers begin. Once you dive in, you may find it so satisfying that you have no need to go any further. Some teachers become so enthralled with crayon resist and the Picturing Writing process that they are content using variations of this process all year.

Collage using hand-painted textured papers, however, offers some advantages that no other two-dimensional medium can provide. First of all, the hand-painted papers themselves are tremendously enjoyable and non-threatening to make. With absolutely no "artistic ability" necessary, everybody (students and teachers alike) will enjoy exploring a variety of simple texturing techniques. This process is guaranteed to entice even the most reluctant learners.

Once created, the portfolios of hand-painted papers offer each student the raw materials for constructing a collage story (or images for writing poetry). This process makes available different kinds of thinking and creative problem-solving opportunities. It also provides students with concrete tools for constructing meaning and developing their story through gluing cut or torn shapes to each page. I can't say enough about the opportunities for rich and diverse thinking this process offers as students move shapes freely on each page before gluing them down. Students are able to rehearse, draft, and revise their stories before ever picking up a pencil to write. Collage offers an extremely rich visual, tactual, and kinesthetic thinking experience, yet as I have mentioned, it is far more involved. For this reason, I usually recommend that teachers begin the year with crayon resist, then move to the more sophisticated processes toward the end of the year if they so choose.

Teachers interested in more fully exploring crayon resist or collage made from hand-painted papers within the framework of fully fleshed-out art-based literacy models (Picturing Writing and Image-Making respectively) can find more information on The Center for the Advancement of Art-Based Literacy Web site: www.picturingwriting.org. Hands-on teacher training along with comprehensive instructional manuals are available for those who wish to explore these processes in depth.

Once teachers understand the ability of art materials and art processes to support imaginative, detailed thinking and to access rich descriptive language, it is difficult for them to return to using the traditional uninspiring media commonly found in the classroom. Be forewarned!

5 Writing

Weaving Pictures into Words

*The pictures paint the words on paper for you
so your words are much better. The words are more descriptive.
Sometimes you can't describe the pictures because they are so beautiful.*

—Serena, Grade 6

We generally acknowledge that a good writer "paints pictures with words." Part of the mystery of crafting a strong piece of writing stems from the difficulty many people have creating a mental image and holding onto it long enough to write about it with any depth and richness. It is nearly impossible to paint a picture with words if you can't picture what you are writing about. Creating actual pictures first gives students concrete visual tools for securing those images on paper before they begin to write—a practice useful to almost all students, and invaluable to those who find writing difficult. Once pictures become affixed to the page, they are there for the looking (reading) and describing.

Creating pictures before writing also provides structured, embedded thinking and rehearsal time as students develop and record their ideas on paper using art materials. In their very engagement in a process that defines them as artists, writers, and crafters of quality picture books, students strengthen their visualization skills. Knowing they are going to be painting pictures regularly, they look more carefully at the world around them, taking "mental snapshots" for later use. They call up those mental images when it is time to paint. Later, they practice visualization skills when they listen to their own or others' writing (whether that of peers or professionals) to determine if the words have painted a picture. They experience the power of transmediation as they stare at a picture while listening to the words that accompany it. As their brains process two languages simultaneously, another sort of visualization occurs: the pictures appear to come to life. All this creates a kind of magic I like to capitalize on in the classroom.

These opportunities to visualize help expand and build visualization skills that support all aspects of literacy learning. My daughter was ten years old when, after having been involved in several painting-and-then-writing book-making projects, she sat down and wrote a vivid passage replete with rich sensory description (the kind that paints a picture in the reader's mind) without having painted first. When I asked her how she came up with such wonderful words (words that were very different from her typical "bare bones" use of language), she told me, "I learned how to paint pictures in my mind." I knew immediately that it was her experiences painting that had helped her to sharpen her visualization skills.

By participating in Artists/Writers Workshop, students naturally become keen observers of the world around them as well as grow more adept at visualizing and retaining images in their minds. This is key to becoming effective writers.

Insight for Teachers

Another advantage to having students' create pictures first before they write is that it opens a window into their minds. For a teacher, sitting down and trying to help a reluctant writer expand a piece of writing can be a very frustrating, and often unsuccessful, exercise. When conferring with a student who is not particularly verbal, or with an English-language learner who may not have a wide vocabulary to draw from, drawing out more information to enrich a piece of writing can be particularly challenging.

The experience is quite different when one or more concrete images sits directly in front of a student, particularly pictures that the student has created and thus has some investment in. At that point, drawing out more information is a matter of asking one simple question: "Can you tell me what is happening in your picture?" Most students can read their pictures to access more detail and description fairly easily. Using pictures as a shared vehicle for conversation, you may discover a surprising depth of thought.

Given tools that allow them to develop their ideas in pictures, students no longer find themselves staring blankly at a blank piece of paper. The images they create give them something to look at and something tangible to talk about and write about. Telling about their pictures (a process I call *reading the picture* or *oral rehearsal*) and writing to their pictures comes naturally to students engaged in art-based writing.

Learning About the Magic of Words: Building Active Vocabulary

Once students have developed their ideas by crafting detailed pictures, the next step is to ensure that their rich, detailed thinking finds its way onto the written page. I have developed a two-pronged strategy to help students make this leap, inviting them to read their pictures aloud to describe what is happening in their pictures, and inviting them to engage in a written brainstorming process using specially designed brainstorming sheets.

Oral Rehearsal

Some of the more verbal students naturally want to tell about their picture or picture sequence by reading their artwork while other students may be reluctant to volunteer. Whether students are quiet or not, it is important to offer all students this opportunity to orally rehearse their story. Reading their pictures—to their teacher or to classmates—helps them reconnect with what they were thinking as they crafted their pictures. It also helps them see more and read more meaning into each picture. As students move from the visual language of their artwork to the verbal language of words, they experience the phenomenon of transmediation, which I first introduced in Chapter Two. As students read their pictures, they are often drawn more deeply into each image they created and, because of this, they are able to access more sensory description—experiencing each image as if they were there. Cooper, grade 3, explains it like this: "Look at the picture for a long time and you kind of get into the picture and feel stuff, like if there was a breeze or something." Taylor, grade 2, shares her story-writing experience: "I liked the part when the snow was slipping off the trees. I could see that happening in my brain, and I could hear it. I got the picture first and then the sound effects afterward."

Not only have I witnessed this phenomenon repeatedly over the years, but our two research studies also documented tremendous increases in the use of sensory description among students participating in the Picturing Writing and Image-Making processes.

Six-year-old Garrett was one of the 555 students participating in our 1997 yearlong evaluation of an art-and-literature-based approach to writing (Appendix A). Notice the rich sensory quality of his language (Figure 5.1) as he writes to his snowman picture (Color Plate M).

When students are invited to rehearse their stories orally, in essence they are being asked to revisit each picture and read it for meaning. They notice more detail and read meaning into that detail. Through their natural ability to make sense of their world, to make meaning, students' stories grow in detail and description. With each new discovery, the plot thickens. And because it is a lot easier to tell about their pictures than to write about them, oral rehearsal provides an important and very natural bridge between the pictures and the written word.

As students orally rehearse their work, it is useful to ask carefully crafted questions to help them notice more detail in their pictures. Once new meaning is discovered, they will naturally want to include it in their thinking and their writing.

Drawing Out Detail and Description Through Questioning

To make sure that students are in fact reading their pictures (as opposed to retelling the story from memory), it helps to ask them to point to each picture as they tell about it, encouraging them to read the important details. This can be modeled for the entire class by tacking up a picture or a series of pictures on the board. (Most often these would be

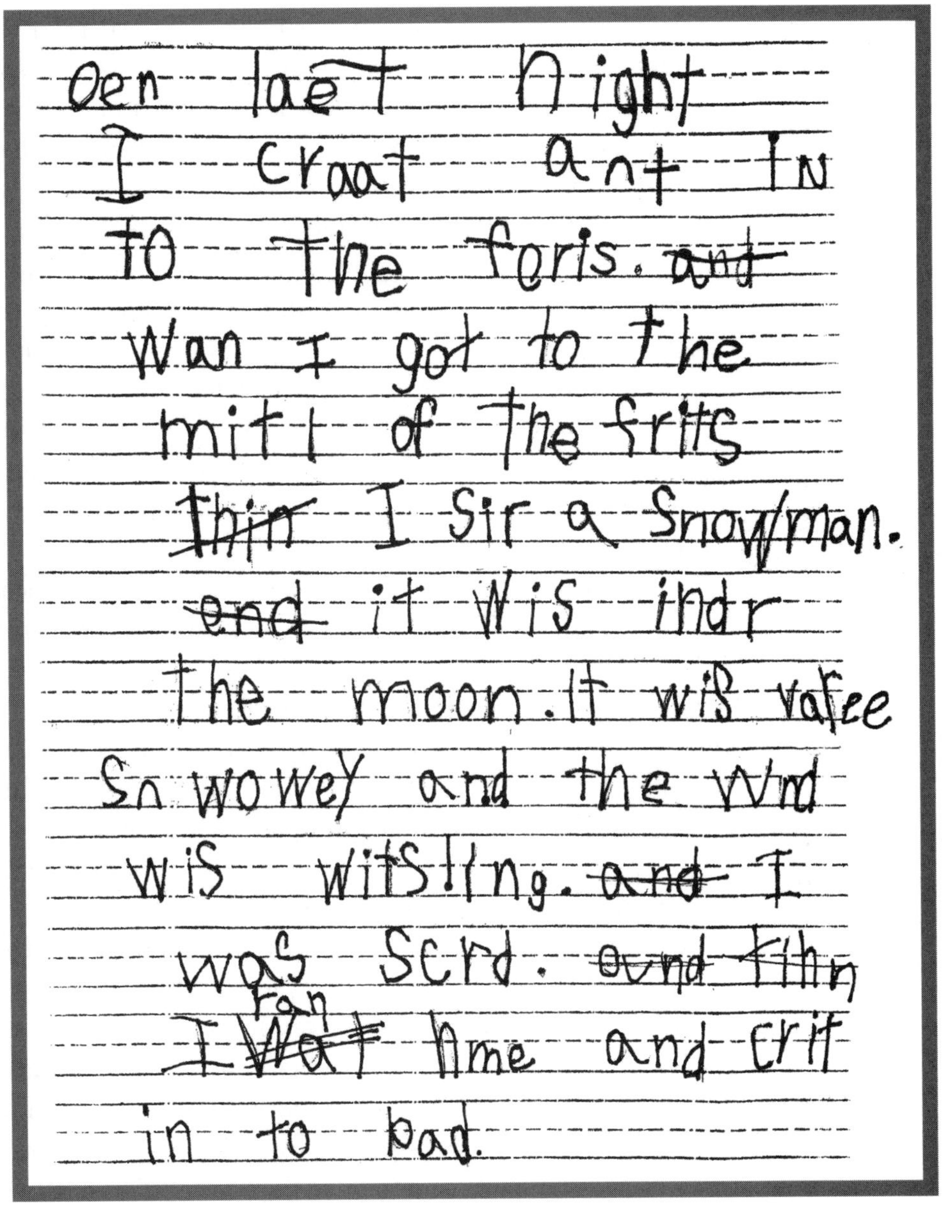

oen laet night
I craat ant In
to the foris. and
wan I got to the
mitt of the frits
thir I sir a snowman.
and it wis indr
the moon. It wis rafee
sn wowey and the wind
wis witsling. and I
was scrd. ound filin
I wat [ran] hme and crit
in to bad.

Figure 5.1.   Garrett's handwritten narrative (The typed version appears with Color Plate M.)

paintings created by the teacher during the Modeling Sessions.) Pointing to each picture, ask: "What is happening in this picture?" and then call on several students (one at a time).

After students, as a group, have taken turns reading the pictures from the class piece (drawing out detail and description), you can invite students to come to the front of the class to read their own picture or picture sequence, thus modeling the same activity using their own work.

Inviting students to tell what is happening in their artwork provides a simple and direct invitation to orally rehearse their words (be it for a single page of writing or an entire story). If you are working with a student who is particularly nonverbal, you may need to support the oral rehearsal process by more direct questioning. Try: "I notice that you made a [noun] in your picture. Can you tell me about it? What is your [noun] doing?" You can ask this question regarding almost anything in the picture, whether it be a character or an object such as a tree, the sun, or even clouds. Through this simple questioning process, you can easily train students to notice the details in the images they have created and help them access detail and descriptive language as they read their pictures.

If you are not sure what exactly a picture is meant to represent, try pointing to a particular object or area of the picture and saying, "Can you tell me about this part of your picture?" (Be careful not to let on that you are not sure what the picture is about.)

As students find words to talk about what may not have been a fully articulated idea, they expand the meaning of the pictures they have created and deepen their thinking. Inviting students to engage in this oral rehearsal process sets the stage for transmediation to occur (the translating of meaning from one sign system to another) as students move from the language of pictures to the language of words. Oral rehearsal enriches the students' meaning-making process, serving to deepen their thinking and enhance their story line.

After some practice, students will begin to internalize this process of attending to the details in their pictures and will not need an outside person to remind them to do this to access detail and description.

On the back of her published book, *The Best Winter of All,* eight-year-old Noami shares her experience of creating pictures first and then revisiting each picture for meaning (Brautigam, 1995):

> I made all my collage pictures first. Then I did my words. It was easier because when I was doing my pictures, I thought about my whole story. Later, when I looked at each picture, I saw more detail. I wrote more because I saw more things to write about.

Crafting Your Questioning for a Purpose

As you become more adept at drawing out information from students using their artwork, you will learn how to craft your questions for a particular purpose. For instance, if you want to support students in developing a sense of setting in their writing, you might ask what I refer to as *setting questions*: "Where does your story take place? What time of day is it? What kind of day is it?" ("Kind of day" can refer to either weather or mood.) "What season is it?" Questions such as these will shift students away from the main character and the action in the story (which is where they tend to focus) to the more subtle setting details. This will encourage them to develop a stronger sense of setting at the beginning of their story.

Similarly, you can enrich both the setting and the story line itself by asking students what I refer to as "the doing question": "Tell me about your [noun]. What is the [same noun] doing?" (For instance, "What is the sun [or the moon] doing?" "What are the clouds doing?") The "doing question" invites the use of strong verbs and will ultimately help students include details in their writing that will make their pictures literally appear to come to life. Jared, grade 2, tells about the magic he witnessed when he read his story out loud as his classmates stared at the pictures: "In my story, when I read it to the class, the animals came to life out of thin air!" Students come to understand that they too can "make magic" if only they include strong verbs in their writing.

Peer Conferences and Small Group Shares

Depending on the age of your students, you may encourage them to work with a partner or in small groups (with or without an overseeing adult) as they practice reading their pictures and orally rehearsing their story lines. Sometimes, to support a peer conference, I have found it helpful to give students "cue cards" that serve as prompts for asking key questions of one another. These cue cards contain key directives or questions such as "Tell me about your setting." "What time of day is it?" "What is the weather?" "What season is it?" "Where does your story take place?" This is obviously an activity geared toward older students. When working with younger students, the oral rehearsal process can be facilitated one-on-one (teacher to student) or in small groups with a facilitating adult (teacher, support staff, or parent volunteer).

Expanding Vocabulary

Hand in hand with the oral rehearsal process comes the purposeful expansion of students' vocabularies, particularly regarding descriptive language. It's simple: if you want your students to paint pictures with words, you need to make sure they have access to a wide palette of colorful language. This is especially easy to accomplish in partnership with integrated curriculum units of study in which the students focus on a common theme. For this very reason, I am a fan of integrated curriculum art-based literacy projects that allow for building a common vocabulary.

Silver Dollar Words

The phrase "silver dollar words" crystallized one day when I brought a silver dollar into a first-grade classroom and passed it around during circle time. The students were eager to hold a real silver dollar. I also passed around a nickel, a coin that was much more familiar to them. We talked about the differences: how rare and special a silver dollar is and how common a nickel is. Most of the children had never seen a silver dollar before. We talked about how hard it is to find silver dollars (even at a bank these days). Students realized that silver dollars are worth a lot more than nickels, not only in actual monetary value but also because silver dollars are harder to find.

I explained that some words, like silver dollars, are a lot more difficult to find than other, more common words. Those words that are harder to find are also a lot more valuable—just like silver dollars. Thus the term *silver dollar words* was created. By contrast, ordinary words— "five-cent words"—are easy to find. They are generally the first words that come to mind. They can serve as placeholders until you can think of a silver dollar word to replace them. One first-grade boy extended the metaphor by noting that, like silver dollars, silver dollar words are usually bigger than five-cent words.

From that day on, the term "silver dollar words" seemed to take hold. The children were very excited by the idea of trying to find silver dollar words. They began coming into the classroom each morning eager to share a new silver dollar word they heard the night before. Students also began identifying silver dollar words during our literature shares or when listening to each other's writing. Students became excited about words! Their excitement only increased when they realized that silver dollar words can make a piece of writing "come alive."

I have since introduced this notion of silver dollar words to students of all ages, and it seems to have a way of catching on. Teachers often remark at students' keen interest in finding silver dollar words to paint a picture that best describe *their* picture. Of course, teachers of older students should use the terms *adjectives, verbs,* and *adverbs* as well as talk about figures of speech such as personification and similes. It is not uncommon to hear teachers remind students to include silver dollar adjectives and silver dollar verbs in their writing.

Word Banks

From a currency of words to a bank is a natural jump. Soon after my first graders and I started talking about words in these terms, we began creating silver dollar word banks, organizing them around particular themes based on our current units of study. I also alphabetized the words in these lists for easy access.

It will be very helpful to your students (of all ages) to have a place to record silver dollar words and to do it in a way that is organized and easy to access. Informal handwritten lists or more formal typed lists—enlarged to post on "word walls" or bound as individual student thesauruses—will support students in their search for just the right word to describe something in their picture. The hope is that students will ultimately internalize these words. Meanwhile, easy external access to the words they have collectively gathered gives them more experience at using them and makes their long-term adoption more likely. When Linda Ball's second graders were creating research-based animal stories within an Artists/Writers Workshop model, they generated lists of pertinent words through movement games and literature-based research. A favorite movement game, designed for the visual and kinesthetic learner, was to have a student act out an animal movement. Classmates needed to guess not what animal the student was imitating but what that animal was *doing*. Under a "How Animals Move" heading, Linda created a word bank as students called out "doing words" to describe their classmates' animal movements. Whether or not students guessed the precise word the actor had in mind, if the word described how animals move, it was written in the word bank. Linda then created an Animal Thesaurus for the students to keep in individual (pocket) writing folders. Within the Animal Thesaurus, Linda created headings such as "Run" or "Walk" and below each heading listed all the words she and her students could think of that painted a better picture of exactly how the animal engaged in each activity. For instance, under "run," Linda listed words such as *scamper, scurry, dart, trot, gallop, lope,* and *charge*. Under "Walk," she listed words such as *amble, lumber, waddle,* and *wander*. Her second graders read through each of the lists, acted out the meaning of each word so as to understand some of the subtle distinctions, and circled the words that pertained to their particular animal. Linda made sure to leave room on each page for students to add to the word lists as they came across pertinent words in their reading. Depending on the unit of study, other word banks may also be relevant. For example, Linda's students created "How Animals Eat" and "Animal Sounds" word banks to accompany "How Animals Move" in their thesaurus.

Using the notion of back planning, a teacher can consider the kinds of words that are going to be most helpful to students and can initiate creating silver dollar word banks that will support students in painting pictures with words during their particular unit of study.

First-grade teacher Gerry Vagos was forced to become inventive about her word banks because her classroom had very little wall space available. She purchased several tri-fold display boards that she could take out and open during writing time and fold up and tuck away when they were not in use.

Typed word lists, which can be added to students' writing folders periodically, will ensure that students have access to an ever-expanding collection of word banks whenever they need them.

Brainstorming Sheets

For some students, the kind of oral rehearsal process described in this chapter, supported by posted word banks and book walks (reading the pictures in picture books as described in Chapter Three), will be enough to ensure they mine their pictures for detail and description. Their experiences may be similar to that of Amanda, a fifth grader who wrote on her About the Artist/Writer page, "I just looked at each picture and wrote what came to mind. As I kept writing, the words just flowed together to make unique descriptions" (Clark, 1995).

For other students, however, words may not flow as easily. Retaining the rich descriptive language that grows out of their artwork may pose a challenge; that rich language seems to vaporize before it finds its way to the written page just as it did for David who told his teacher, "The words fly out of my head before I can get them down on paper" (Chapter One). Additionally, few classes have time enough for every student to orally rehearse every piece of writing even once, let alone as often as might be useful to refine the work. For these reasons, I have developed brainstorming sheets as a way to retrieve, record, and preserve the rich descriptive language embedded in students' artwork. When I began to recognize the potential for students' artwork to generate rich descriptive language, I initiated a "brainstorming process" in which I taped up one of my own modeling pieces of art to the board and asked students to call out describing words. Students were able to access descriptive language about different things in the picture and I recorded their words on the board or on a piece of chart paper. It was during a teacher workshop in Honolulu, when I was modeling my original free-form brainstorming process, that Chris Kapololu—a much more organized colleague—suggested that we identify some of the "important things" we see in the picture and then brainstorm words in columns beneath each noun. Thus the brainstorming sheet—which has gone through many refinements since that time—was born.

The brainstorming sheet provides another layer of scaffolding to ensure that students read each of their pictures to access descriptive language, and that the rich descriptive language mined from each picture finds its way to the written page. It requires students to look at each picture more deeply, read it for detail and description, and then record their descriptive language on paper—the very same piece of paper they will be writing their sentences on.

Using Brainstorming Sheets

The most basic brainstorming sheet is a simple four-column open-ended form designed to activate deep looking and reading of each picture. The top half of the sheet (of letter-size paper held horizontally) consists of brainstorming columns, and the bottom half consists of writing lines.

With brainstorming sheet in hand and picture propped up in a desktop easel stand, students are asked to identify four important *things* (nouns) they see in their picture. Each of the artists, of course, must decide which things in a picture are most important based on their own understanding of the image and what meaning they are hoping to draw out with their words. The next step is to write these four nouns, one in each box at the top of each of the four columns on the brainstorming sheet. (This process is modeled on the DVD Artists/Writers Workshop Overview during the Work Session in the writing strand.)

Students then brainstorm adjectives ("describing words"), verbs ("doing words"), and in some cases, adverbs ("how words") in the column beneath each noun. Sometimes students will try to write sentences in each column, but the system is really designed for single words or short phrases. Figure 5.2 shows a brainstorming sheet filled out by a third-grade student.

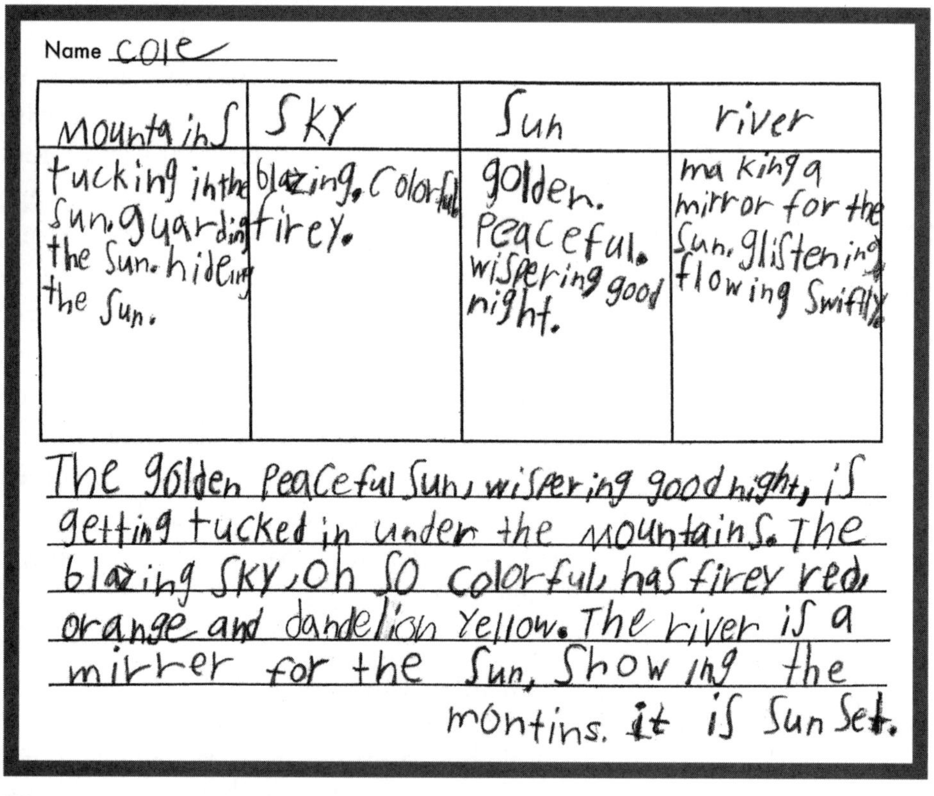
Name cole

mountains	sky	sun	river
tucking in the sun. guarding the sun. hiding the sun.	blazing. colorful firey.	golden. peaceful. wispering good night.	making a mirror for the sun. glistening flowing swiftly

The golden peaceful sun, wispering good night, is getting tucked in under the mountains. The blazing sky, oh so colorful, has firey red, orange and dandelion yellow. The river is a mirrer for the sun, showing the montins. it is sun set.

Figure 5.2. Completed brainstorming sheet.

Source: Brainstorming sheet (blank) is from *Picturing Writing: Fostering Literacy Through Art®* Time of Day Copyright © 1998, Beth Olshansky.

Once students have filled out their brainstorming sheets, they are ready to write. The brainstorming sheet—with half a page of space for brainstormed words and half a page for writing—is designed to make sure that when students are ready to write, all their good ideas are right in front of them.

As in the oral rehearsal process, students using brainstorming sheets learn to look more deeply into their pictures, identify important details, and internalize questions that will help them access descriptive language. I like to begin the brainstorming process with "the doing question," because strong verbs help produce a strong piece of writing. The question for accessing strong verbs ("doing words") is "What is my [noun] doing?" The question for accessing adverbs ("how words") is "How is the [noun] [verb]ing?" For instance, ask, "How is the snow falling?" Possible responses might include *gently, softly, quietly, silently, furiously,* and so on. The question for accessing adjectives ("describing words") is "How would I describe my [noun]?"

Depending on the age of your students and the focus of your mini-lesson, it's useful to emphasize one or more of these questions. Years of personal experience lead me to believe that if I had to focus on only one of these questions, I would choose the "doing question." "What is my [noun] doing?" This will remind students to use strong verbs in their writing. I also like to emphasize this question because too much emphasis on adjectives can result in writing that is overly laden with adjectives and cumbersome to read.

This brainstorming process can be used most effectively to prepare students for writing descriptive passages, poetry, or stories. Over the years, I have customized brainstorming sheets for specific purposes. During a mini-lesson on what makes a strong lead paragraph, for instance, after analyzing a few quality leads, teacher and students might create a class list of the kinds of information authors include in a lead paragraph. Teachers would then create a brainstorming sheet that reminds students to read their pictures for certain kinds of information, in this case weather, season, time of day, a "setting detail," place (where?), and character, as shown in Figure 5.3. (Some leads include the character and some do not. Some lead sentences include just a hint of the character to be introduced on the next page. The lead sentence sheet pictured here shows evidence that the teacher offered her students a literature-based mini-lesson that analyzed the job of the lead sentences.

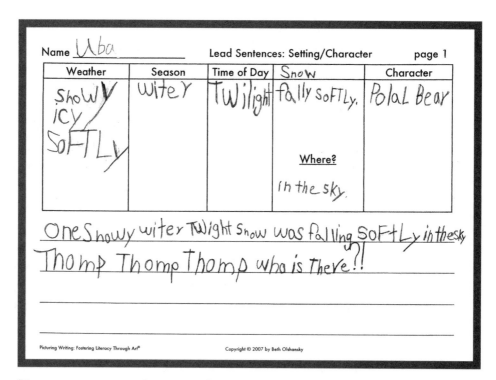

Figure 5.3.   Lead sentence brainstorming sheet completed by second-grade English language learner.

(Clearly this ELL [English language learner] second grader has taken to heart the idea of including only a hint of his character—a hook—on his first page.)

While younger students, English language learners, and other students who struggle with words may use the brainstorming sheet as a reminder to read their picture and write one or two words per column, older students use the brainstorming sheet to generate longer lists of descriptive words and phrases. In that case, it helps to encourage students to revisit their brainstorming sheets and circle the words that *paint the best picture of their picture.* This process of selection is vital to the writing process. It reinforces the notion that effective writers carefully select words and craft their language to paint a picture for the reader. A common misuse of the brainstorming sheet occurs when students include too many adjectives in their writing. When this occurs, encourage students to revise their writing by selecting only those words that do the very best job describing their picture and eliminating the rest. The brainstorming process should help students to thoughtfully craft their writing. Revision (discussed in Chapter Six) takes on a very different light when students are being asked to fine-tune and eliminate extra words rather than add to an existing skeletal text.

As students work to craft their own words, one criterion for their writing can be: "Have I used words that paint a picture?" While first grader Steven told us that in Artists/Writers Workshop he learned how to paint pictures in Mrs. Rafferty's mind, Serena, a sixth grader, reflected on her experiences during Artists/Writers Workshop: "The pictures paint the words on paper for you, so your words are much better. The words are more descriptive. Sometimes you can't describe your pictures because they are so beautiful!"

Reflecting on the Brainstorming Process

The brainstorming sheet is specifically designed to provide a bridge between the picture and the written word. As students choose the four most important things they see in their pictures and begin the process of describing them through brainstorming words that "tell what each thing is doing," they are drawn deeper into their picture. They move from thinking using a visual language or sign system to thinking using a verbal one. In the process of recasting meaning from one sign system to another, they discover new meanings and sometimes make surprising observations and discoveries.

Because the act of filling out brainstorming sheets requires students to look more deeply into each picture, it also stimulates seeing and connecting with the image in a way that might otherwise not occur. Filling out brainstorming sheets requires students to assign written words to various parts of their visual image. This forces them to experience the phenomenon of transmediation, or the recasting of meaning from one sign system to another. While this may first occur when students read their pictures during oral rehearsal, filling out the brainstorming sheet makes this seeing and meaning-making process more tangible and concrete. As students move from reading their pictures to writing down words via the brainstorming process, they not only discover but also record new meanings. This is part of the ongoing magic I witness in the classroom.

The mental processing required to move from thinking in pictures to thinking in words engages much more of the brain than when students just write, and different kinds of thought processes (visual *and* verbal) are stimulated. Thus this exercise makes more complete use of the students' capacity to think. Whether or not all students have the opportunity to read their pictures and orally rehearse to the class or to a partner, asking students to fill out brainstorming sheets gives them the opportunity to deepen their meaning-making as well as to access more detail and descriptive language. It is important to remember that the brainstorming process serves as an invitation for deep looking, expanded meaning making, and vocabulary expansion. The brainstorming sheet also acts as a sensory integrator, connecting the visual with other sensory experiences. In that filling out the brainstorming sheet requires that students look more deeply into their picture and come up with describing words to tell about it, the brainstorming sheet and the act of deep looking it inspires serves to literally draw students into their pictures in a very real way. This happened for six-year-old Garrett as he stared into what appeared to be a typical first-grade painting of a snowman (described earlier in this chapter). Drawn into his picture by the color and details he had created, Garrett began to tap his own pool of sensory memories about being outside at night in the winter.

Garrett shared his experience writing to his piece: "I wanted to show a scary, wicked cold night. When I was painting, my snowman turned blue and I didn't like it. But it made the night look more scary. I could just picture a person outside in the scary night under the moon. I got a feeling for a scary night, then I got the words, then I just wrote." (See Color Plate M.) What Garrett tells us is consistent with the results of our initial research study, conducted in 1991–1993, and our later research in 1997–1998, when we documented far more sensory description in the writing of those first- and second-grade students who were participating in our art-based writing methods as compared to a demographically matched group who were participating in more traditional approaches to writing.

Why Improvement in Writing?

With the ongoing sharing of literature and study of the author's craft, the emphasis on identifying "silver dollar words" and building community word banks, oral rehearsal, and the structured brainstorming of descriptive language to tell about the pictures, Artists/Writers

Workshop is designed to greatly enhance students' vocabularies, their use of descriptive language, and their wordsmithing abilities. While all the scaffolding built in around word study is apparent, I cannot emphasize enough the value of creating art before writing. Hannah, a third grader and seasoned participant in Artists/Writers Workshop, said it best: "I always make my pictures first because then I can get looks at them to help me with my describing words. If I wrote my words first, I wouldn't be able to see my describing words in my pictures."

It is important to keep in mind that in its very design and daily practice, the art-first approach described in this book eliminates the established classroom bias that favors the verbal learner—without disadvantaging verbal learners in the process. The words still matter and are very much a focus of enriching the meaning-making process. Yet, by giving all students access to visual and kinesthetic, as well as verbal modes of thinking at each and every step of the writing process, teachers level the playing field so that students whose strengths lie outside the verbal realm can enthusiastically engage in solid literacy practice. This multi-modal approach supports them in the acquisition of essential reading and writing skills, and it is just the hook they need to become engaged and remain engaged and motivated learners. This means that all students have the tools they need to succeed, and therefore are able to experience themselves as capable, creative human beings. And don't forget, the impact of this dual language, art-first approach is greatly enhanced by the phenomenon of transmediation, which serves to deepen students' mental processing, engaging them in higher-order thinking as they become immersed in moving back and forth between pictures and words (Cowan and Albers, 2006; Siegel, 1995).

Beyond this overall re-visioning of the way writing instruction is delivered and in order to provide teachers with a simple, effective format for supporting their diverse learners, for those interested I have developed fully fleshed-out, comprehensive units of study. These provide students and teachers with ongoing, carefully designed progressions of art-infused, literature-based writing mini-lessons designed not only to engage reluctant learners but also to teach specific literary elements through multiple modalities. Delivered in a simple, user-friendly format, these mini-lessons recognize, apply, and capitalize on the parallel and complementary languages of pictures and words. (A small sampling of these mini-lessons appear in Chapter Nine, with a full listing of instructional materials and manuals available at www.picturingwriting.org.)

Within the Artists/Writers Workshop approach, students build a solid foundation of understanding as they continually apply newly acquired skills to the crafting of their own quality picture books. To the best of my knowledge, no other approach to literacy learning offers such an intricately designed, fully developed system for teaching writing to all kinds of learners.

6 Refining and Celebrating the Work

You check it over and . . . um . . . you say this isn't right and you check it over like a hundred times, and then you finally found the right word or the right sentence, and then when you are done, you get that like proud feeling.

—Savannah, Grade 3

Once students have crafted words that paint pictures, they have a special treat in store: the magic of witnessing what active verbs and sensory description do to the actual pictures they've created. Jared, one of Linda Ball's second graders, was the first in his class to try to articulate the magic he experienced: "When I was reading my story to the class, I was really thinking really hard . . . and the pictures came out of my mind. They came to life, and they just acted what I was reading." In fact, all Jared's classmates will tell you that if you include silver dollar action words in your writing, when you stare at the picture while someone reads the words, "It makes the picture come alive." How do they know this? They have witnessed it with their very own eyes.

When asked to explain "the magic trick," Linda's students launch into a variety of explanations: Kelsey struggles to get the phrasing right: "Well, we believed that was a real picture because we thought it was a real picture because it IS like a real picture—so we imagined it and then it came to life." Katelyn insists, "It's like Harry Potter." Jared steps in to explain, "We 'imagined' the clouds and stuff moving. When you told the story it made our minds think of a movie we were watching that made the clouds and everything move." Without knowing any of the research data, Jared is tapping into the very root of comprehension: the ability of words to bring pictures (actual or mental) to life.

Once students experience the magic of bringing words and pictures together and discuss how "the magic trick" works, they can be invited to make magic with their own pictures. They join an elite circle of wordsmiths and illusionists, magicians who possess coveted knowledge about how to make pictures come alive. It is hard to resist wanting to try your hand at making magic with the pictures you've created. "Making magic" can also become a criterion for assessment. During the Group Share, when students gather around the Artists Frame to view each other's art work in relation to the writing that accompanies it, one criterion can be, "Did Jared's words make his picture come to life?"

In my experience, students never tire of the magic trick and seeing if the words make the picture appear to "come alive." They settle themselves readily and become perfectly still (and silent) in order to see if a classmate's words make the picture come to life.

Recently, in Merrilee Thissell's first-grade classroom in an inner-city school, students gathered on the rug to share the lead sentences they had written to go with their lead pictures. Students stared intently at Hailee's painting as she read her lead sentences. Her classmates could not contain themselves from spontaneously calling out, "I saw the magic! I saw the magic!" When Merrilee settled down her students and asked them to engage in a discussion about what just happened, one of her first graders remarked, "When I heard Hailee's words, it made her picture come alive! I saw her snow falling and her trees blowing." There followed a chorus of "Me too, me too!" In her reflections at the back of her published book, Hailee wrote, "I like to write this way because I get to paint first. I look at my painting and think of silver dollar words to tell about it . . . I stared at my painting and my words made magic."

Revision and Editing

Revision and editing are important parts of any writing process. Most students are reluctant to revise their writing. But when revision and editing are presented as preparation for publishing the art and writing that students have worked so hard on (and have established such strong emotional ties with), revision becomes meaningful and purposeful. Students are eager to see their literary and artistic masterpieces completed and published. Because of the exceptional nature of students' artwork and the literature-based mini-lessons that strengthen their writing, these published pieces will indeed be something students are proud of. In fact, they often become family keepsakes. I know this because I occasionally run into former elementary school students, some of whom are now six feet tall and tower over me. Every single one of these now high school or even college-age students has told me that they still have the books they made. Recently, in a college course I taught at the University of New Hampshire, one of my graduate students came to class flaunting the Image-Making book she made in first grade!

Given the emotional attachments students have to this work, herein lies a golden opportunity to introduce revision and editing in a way that is difficult to resist: the opportunity to make sure that students' own labors of love are indeed just the way they want them before they are made permanent and become keepsakes forever and ever.

Seven-year-old Connor offered this about his experiences making his book in first grade, "I worked really hard on it and if there was something I didn't like, I tried again. And then if that wasn't good, I tried again. I kept on trying until I got it *exactly* how I wanted it." (You can see and hear Connor and his classmates reflect on their experiences in the first video clip at www.picturingwriting.org/videos.html.)

Revision

Ask any teacher. Most students do not like to revise their writing. They see it as arduous and a nuisance. The revision process within Artists/ Writers Workshop is quite different, and students feel differently about it. First of all, because students are working in two languages, the language of pictures and the language of words, revision can occur within their art as well as within their writing. As a result of discussions held during the Artists Share, students may decide to add details to their pictures. This, in turn, may cause them to want to revise their writing. Occasionally, students may decide that an entire picture needs to be redone; they usually welcome the opportunity to paint some more. Sometimes students end up rearranging the order of their pictures within their story sequence or making a new picture and placing the original one on the cover. With the definition of literary work broadened to include pictures as well as words, the activities that revision encompasses also change. Once students experience the satisfaction of improving their artwork, they understand the value of revision and are more open to revising their writing. As Ellen, a second grader participating in Artists/ Writers Workshop, explains, "I got to make revisions on my pictures and a few revisions, well, on my story. After you do it, you feel quite happy."

While revision can address improvements in the pictures, it can also address more traditional attention to written text. Even then, this revision process differs from what teachers and students are accustomed to. As noted in Chapter Five, the art-centered process gives teachers options that are far more effective—and far more rewarding for both parties— than staring at a piece of bare-bones writing and trying to elicit further detail and description from a student. Teachers have new tools and more options. They can ask students to review the lists of words and phrases that appear on their brainstorming sheets to remind them of their earlier thinking, or they can ask students to revisit their pictures, inviting them once again to read each picture to tell what is happening on each page. The questioning process outlined in Chapter Five for oral rehearsal will come in handy during the revision process as well, as a way of encouraging students to flesh out more detail and description in their pictures. Sometimes, as was the case with Greg, a simple compliment or invitation to "Tell me about your picture" was enough to elicit some wonderful language and an expansion of the story line:

Greg was a capable writer but would much rather be doing something else with his time. Indeed, he was always the first of his second-grade class to finish anything, no matter what the task.

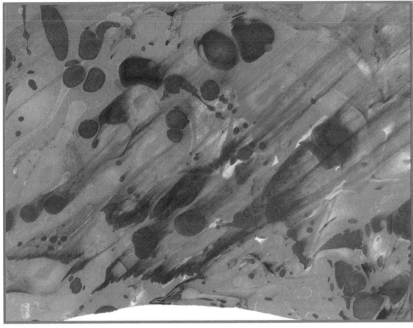

It seems like we are caught in a meteor shower. I go outside. Huge rocks like pumpkins hit me from all sides. It is raining rocks.

Color Plate A   David, grade 2

I know someone special. Only I can see him. He comes out at night. He seems to glow at me. He swishes through the trees. He slithers through the grass. He makes ripples in the water and he blows in the wind.

Color Plate B   Jamie, grade 1

He's not the swan who swims and drinks from the silver lake. He's not the wind snake who glides with the wind. He's not the great bear paw that belongs to the bear of the wild. He's not the beautiful flower with one leaf and the sweetest of nectar. He's not the sparkling purple rock.

Color Plate C   Jamie, grade 1

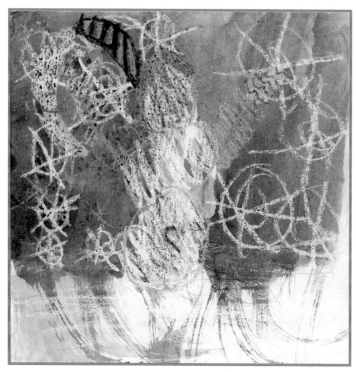

One quiet and silent night, a raccoon sat on my snowman's head. A white owl hooted in a whisper. The moon smiled. The snowflakes fell more quietly than ever before. Drooom went the clock. The clock struck midnight and the stars sprinkled away.

Color Plate D   Chris, grade 1

Day slowly awakens. She lazily opens one eye, pushing royal purples high into the sky, leaving the teals and aquas to linger. A tree stands alone with no one to turn to on a barren landscape. Finally, day reaches a warm hand to touch the hard frozen ground.

Color Plate E   Reilly, grade 5

Color Plate F   Meghan, grade 1

Snowflakes dance
like winter angels
in the deep dark night.

Color Plate G   Devin, grade 1

Big black shark
Swimming in stormy waters.
Likes the foamy waves!

Jagged orange lighting fights
in the dark purple sky.
Emerald green ocean
sends crashing waves
to the sandy shore,
leaving treasures behind.

Color Plate H   Emilee, grade 1

Sarena lived in the green
grassy fields of Ireland
that fluttered in the wind
like butterfly wings.
When the wind swirled
over the hilltops, the
green grass swayed like
waves rolling into the bay.

Color Plate J   Amanda, grade 6

The giant hand cast
her out into the lake
with a splash.

Color Plate J   Kelsea, grade 4

A large sunset-colored
salmon came along and
gulped her down whole.

Color Plate K   Kelsea, grade 4

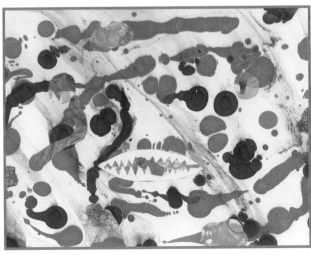

Inside the sunset salmon,
she felt sick. . . . She squirmed
over to one eye and peeked out
as if it were a window.

Color Plate L   Kelsea, grade 4

One late night, I crept out of my house into the forest. When I got to the middle of the forest, I saw a snowman. It was sitting under the moon. It was very snowy and the wind was whistling. I was scared. I ran home and crept into bed.

Color Plate M   Garrett, grade 1

The scuba diver saw lots of jellyfish. They were big and round, bumpy and slimy. They had big purple dots in the middle. They were squirting ink into the bottom of the ocean. When the scuba diver looked up, he saw the sunlight shining down through the water.

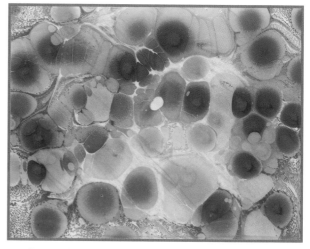

Color Plate N   Greg, grade 2

Color Plate O   Andrew, grade 3

Shhh! The golden sun is going to sleep as it slowly turns off its light. The mountains are shading the sun so the day can turn into night. The river is changing colors as it flows slowly. The sky is bright and colorful.

Color Plate P

Honda uses a close-up, increased texture, and cool, dark colors to heighten drama.

Color Plate Q

While the colors remain cool, the absence of texture creates a sense of calm.

Color Plate R

Honda's dramatic change to warm colors creates a sense of relief.

Color Plate S

Final mid-range view serves to distance reader. Warm colors convey a happy ending.

Color Plate T

Silvio, grade 3

One windy summer night, a fox pup wandered away from his den in a tree trunk at the edge of the forest. The hungry pup was searching for food. As he sniffed the air, he heard a rock fall. He started to shiver. He felt scared.

Color Plate U   Jared, grade 2

Suddenly, he came out to an open field where there was a coyote that was hungrily staring at the pup with his golden eyes. The starving coyote was ready to charge at the young pup.

Color Plate V   Jared, grade 2

Greg decided to construct a story about a scuba diver based on an abundance of blue marbleized papers he made, which reminded him of the ocean, and a purple and magenta marbleized paper he'd forgotten to comb, which reminded him of jellyfish. Greg constructed his collage story, image by image. When it came time for him to show the scuba diver's encounter with a school of jellyfish, he decided to use his "jellyfish paper" whole as it was perfect just the way it was. He finished constructing his story and then sat down to write. Predictably, he dashed off his written story in no time and announced he was done. For his favorite jellyfish page, he had written, "He saw lots of jellyfish."

When conferring with Greg, I commented on how much I loved the paper on his jellyfish page. (See Color Plate N.) He immediately got excited and began telling me all about his jellyfish, how they were big and slimy and had purple ink inside of them that they could squirt out into the ocean. I told Greg that those were some wonderful descriptions, and I wondered out loud if he thought his readers might like to know more about his jellyfish. Greg agreed that it was a good idea and easy enough for him to add because he had a record of his thoughts right in front of him in his picture. He took his collage story back to his desk and revised that page to read:

"The scuba diver saw lots of jellyfish. They were big and round, bumpy and slimy. They had big purple dots in the middle. They were squirting ink into the bottom of the ocean. When the scuba diver looked up, he saw the sunlight shining down through the water."

The sunlight was something Greg hadn't mentioned before. I was curious how he had come up with such a wonderful sensory description, so during the Group Share, I asked him if he could tell his classmates where he got the idea for that wonderful language about the sunlight shining *down through the water. Greg grinned and said, "It was easy. I saw it in my picture."*

This vignette serves as an important reminder of the value of encouraging students to read their pictures over and over again. Had Greg not been invited to reread his picture, he never would have noticed the sunlight shining down through the water and that wonderful image would never have found his way into his writing. This experience is not uncommon, and once again, it offers an example of the power of transmediation. Also note the sensory quality to his description, which Greg could have only achieved by picturing himself there, in the story.

I worked with Greg years before I developed the brainstorming sheets and process. Now that students are encouraged to engage in that additional layer of scaffolding, to fill out their brainstorming sheet before they draft their text (which forces them to read their pictures), some teachers face new kinds of revision challenges. In contrast to the typical revision process in which teachers are encouraging students to add to their writing, students engaged in the brainstorming process may find themselves having to take away, to edit out excessive "silver dollar words." At times, students have so much descriptive language at their fingertips from reading their pictures and brainstorming silver dollar words that they have a hard time selecting words. Sometimes students try to include all their silver dollar words despite the circling and selection process described in Chapter Five. In this case, teachers should encourage their students to revisit their pictures once again and select the very best words to capture precisely what they are describing. As students learn how to be selective, they also come to understand that revision is an important part of the writer's craft.

Color Coding

Color coding is another concrete revision activity available to teachers and students. It offers yet another layer of scaffolding for those who need it.

For students who are already familiar with parts of speech, teachers can set up a color-coding system for adjectives, verbs, and adverbs. (Each part of speech would be identified by a different color.) For instance, you might have students read through their writing and underline all the adjectives with red, the strong verbs with green, and the adverbs with blue. Only silver dollar verbs should be underlined, so verbs such as *is, was, went, goes,* and so on do not warrant being underlined. Once students' writing has been color-coded, students can ask questions like these:

✦ Did I include any adjectives?

✦ Did I include too many adjectives (too many underlines of the same color in a row)?

✦ Did I include strong verbs?

✦ Did I include any adverbs?

✦ Do I have a balance of colored underlines on my page (as opposed to only one color, for instance)?

✦ Do all three colors appear on my page?

Students should be able to glance at their color-coded writing to answer these basic questions and then revise their writing accordingly.

Through this color-coding activity students often discover that they need to be more selective with their use of adjectives (having used too many adjectives on a page), or that they have forgotten to use strong verbs, or neglected to include any adverbs. An activity as simple as finding a place for an adverb can enhance a piece of writing. Listen to the difference between "The sun rises over the bay" and "The sun rises silently over the bay." Adverbs often serve to enhance the mood in a piece of writing.

Younger students can be asked to underline or highlight their "describing" and "doing words" using one or two colors depending on their ability. Emergent writers may be asked to use a yellow marker to highlight their silver dollar words. With sensitivity toward what is grade-level appropriate, highlighting or color coding words gives students visual tools to evaluate and refine their use of descriptive language.

Of course, revision goes well beyond the measures described here. Just as quality literature is used to inspire good writing during the drafting stage, quality literature can be used to inspire revision. Of course, the more students read and are read to, the more they internalize the sound of a compelling piece of writing. Elements such as voice, mood, the development of dramatic tension, a sense of relief, and conclusion become part and parcel with immersion and analysis of quality literature. The oral rehearsal process can also be helpful in the process of revision.

Not only can students mine their images for detail and description, but they can also experiment with voice during the oral rehearsal process.

Once students have revised their writing, they are ready to begin the editing process.

Editing

Language mechanics need to be taught but often the process can be dry and unappealing. Once again, the prospect of publishing their very own exceptional picture books gives students a good reason to want to get it right. The story they have labored over and established an emotional connection to is about to be published. What more incentive for engagement could a student ask for? Skeptics may say that writing process teachers have been publishing books for decades. This is true. But wait until you see the exceptional literary and artistic masterpieces that students create. You will understand what I am talking about.

An editing worksheet can be developed with grade-level-appropriate expectations in mind. These would provide guidelines for editing. For emergent writers or students with special learning needs, an individualized editing worksheet can provide individual students with written expectations. Everyone can participate in the editing process to the best of their ability.

Editing can be made even more engaging by presenting it as a formal activity. To support the editing process, Linda Ball decided to open a publishing house in her second-grade classroom on the day her students were to begin editing their stories. When they came to school that morning, they found a sign on the classroom door: Mrs. Ball's Publishing House. As her students entered the classroom, she addressed them formally as Ms. Jones or Mr. Smith (whatever their last name happened to be) and asked them to please hang up their coats and sharpen their pencils. "We have very important work to do today." She also distributed newly sharpened color pencils. Linda welcomed her staff into the editing room and explained how they were about to undertake an exciting publishing project. As the president of the company, she would be providing them with company training and then would ask them all to perform their jobs, preparing their stories for publication.

Linda showed her students how to use a few simple editing symbols. She had crafted some writing of her own that typified some common weaknesses among her students' writing and used this as a training tool—among the problems it featured were inconsistent verb tense, lack of subject-verb agreement, extraneous "ands" and "thens," misspelled words, and lack of proper punctuation and capitalization. After students practiced editing her piece as part of the company training, the publishing house officially opened operations. Students were given an editing checklist to help guide their efforts and eagerly went to work.

Typing

Older students can be invited to type their stories on school computers. This presents a whole new opportunity to scrutinize their work as well as make choices about font size, style, layout, and so on. I remember the day fifth-grade teacher Millie Parks took her students into the computer lab to type up their Picturing Writing stories. The students were so excited that they raced around the room frenetically checking in with each other about proper punctuation, grammar, and even word choice. I had never seen such attunement to grammatical details in the classroom or such excitement about editing.

If students aren't old enough to type their own pieces, teachers can either ask for parent volunteers or type the books themselves. Some teachers have told me how much they value the opportunity to review their students' work as they type. Other teachers would just a soon have one or more parent volunteers do the typing. Parent volunteers should be given specific guidelines for typing if you want your students' books to come out looking a certain way. After all the work that the students have put into these literary and artistic masterpieces, they should be typed and published with care.

Preparing for Publishing

Whether or not students, parents, or teachers type students' work, it is important that the work be thoroughly proofread for errors. There is nothing more disappointing than getting a published book back with typos or grammatical errors. Some may argue that if students type their own work, it should reflect their ability. Or if students are editing their own work, the published piece should contain the remaining grammatical or spelling errors. I disagree. When spelling or grammatical errors remain in a published piece—which will be read and reread over and over again—it only serves to imprint improper conventions in students' minds. Like it or not, every publishing house works very hard to make sure that published pieces do not contain mistakes. If teachers are concerned about giving families a record of their child's work, I recommend sending home students' rough drafts in a folder. I think this is a good practice in any case.

Honoring and Celebrating

It is important to acknowledge and honor students for all the hard work and care they have put into their finished art and writing. Because students work in such earnest to craft their literary masterpieces, it is important to honor and celebrate both the process and the results. You can honor their process through providing the time and support students need to create fine work, along with opportunities for them to share both their work and their experience throughout the process. It is a simple matter to add a few basic props to the Group Share that serve to make the sharing process that much more memorable for students and help to capture the students' full attention.

Artists Frame

The first and most useful prop is the Artists Frame, a simple, hand-made device that holds and displays the art during the Group Share. The frame serves to honor the work of art and, of course, its creator. A simple version (described in detail in Appendix B), provides a thick black line around the piece of art being discussed. Students have said that the Artists Frame "makes the picture look special," "makes the picture stand out," and "frames the painting." While it honors each student's work, it also provides a visual focus during the sharing process. Student art somehow looks more "finished" when it is placed in this simple black-box frame. (The Artists Frame can be seen in the DVD

Artists/Writers Workshop Overview during the two sections on the Group Share.)

Artists/Writers Chair

Hand-in-hand with the Artists Frame is the Artists/Writers Chair, a seat of honor occupied by the student whose work is being discussed. The rest of the class sits on the floor in front of the Artists Frame. The chair is placed at the back of the group or circle so that the featured student can easily view the displayed art work along with the rest of the class. (This differs from the traditional writing workshop in which the author's chair is placed at the front of the room.) Occasionally students hop out of the Artists/Writers Chair in order to point to a specific area in their painting or other work of art.

Appendix B also provides detailed information on both the Artists Frame and the Artists/Writers Chair.

Publishing with Care

You can also honor student work by making every effort to publish their work with care. Students are often amazed when they see their published books for the first time—all of a sudden, they *see* what they have created!

Grayson, a third grader, captures this sentiment vividly at the very end of the Artists/Writers Workshop Overview on the DVD:

> I can't wait to see what this book looks like when I look back
> in like two, three, or four years from now, see what it looks like
> and then like "I wrote that? Wow! I didn't know!" I just . . .
> I think . . . I think it's the best I have felt in a long time.

On a lighter note, six-year-old Melissa, a readiness first grader responded spontaneously when she was first handed her very own published collage book: "I can't believe that a child actually made this book."

Once student work has been published, it is important to give students a chance to celebrate their accomplishment through sharing it with family and friends. Many teachers and schools like to hold some sort of literary event as well as inviting students to share their work within the classroom. Celebrating student work can take many forms, including during-school, after-school, or evening events that parents, siblings, grandparents, and community members are invited to attend. Sometimes students are invited to be "guest artists/writers" in other classrooms within their school building. In one local school, first graders took their published stories to the middle school to read them to the seventh graders during their language arts period. The middle school students were duly impressed and were then inspired to create their own picture books.

Gold Seals: Everyone's Work is Honored

While all students are proud of the work they create during Artists/ Writers Workshop, for at-risk learners, having the chance to share their work and be honored for their accomplishments can be of particular importance to their self-esteem and growing sense of what they are capable of producing. I often buy serrated gold seals that I place on the protective covers of students' newly published books (similar to what one sees on the Caldecott Award–winning books). I remember the first time I decided to place gold seals on students' published books, I was in a first-grade classroom. After borrowing several Caldecott Award–winning books from the school library, I gave a mini-lesson on the Caldecott Award. I explained to students what an honor it is to receive one. We looked through several books and discussed why the students thought that these particular books were chosen. I told them that usually only one illustrator in the whole world receives a Caldecott Award each year. But this year, at their school, we had to break that rule. Each person would receive an award. The children spontaneously burst into a round of applause. As they came up to receive their published books, I placed a gold seal (available at your local office supply store) on the clear plastic cover and then shook each student's hand, congratulating each child. Some of these first graders were literally trembling with excitement.

Three months later, I found myself once again at the front of the same class ready to hand out another batch of newly published books. Ryan, a first grader with thick glasses and multiple learning issues, timidly raised his hand, "Are we breaking the rules again?" When I assured him that we were indeed breaking the rules again, that every student would receive an award, the students once again burst into a spontaneous round of applause.

Ten years later, I found myself standing before a third-grade classroom about to place gold seals on a batch of newly published books. The students had worked very hard on these books—both on their art and on their writing. I published their books with care as a thank-you to the students for all their hard work.

One third-grade student, Andrew, had had a challenging year and a particularly tough morning. Prior to my handing out the students' beautifully handcrafted books, I had observed Andrew working on a math paper. He became so frustrated trying to complete this worksheet that he crumpled his paper into a ball and began jamming his pencil into his desktop. His frustration was palpable. He was beside himself as he sat in his chair holding back tears.

When it came time for me to hand out the students' published books, I called them up to the front of the classroom, one at a time, to shake their hand and place a gold seal on each student's book. When Andrew came up to receive his book, he barely looked at me. A dark cloud still hung over him. He carried his newly published book back to his seat and flung it on his desk, not even bothering to open it. Clearly he was still feeling miserable. Recalling a particularly stunning painting Andrew had made, I walked over to him and knelt down beside him. "Andrew," I whispered as I flipped open his book to the very first page. "Do you remember making this painting? This is one of the most amazing paintings I have ever seen." Andrew glanced at his picture and then immediately burst into tears. "Andrew, what's wrong?" I pleaded, convinced I had done something terribly wrong. Sobbing and gasping for air, he wailed, "These . . . are . . . are tears . . . of . . . of joy . . . I didn't think . . . I could do . . . *anything* anymore." With that truth-telling, Andrew uncontrollably wept "tears of joy" having now seen living proof of the talents he had long lost sight of. (See Color Plate O.)

7   Planning, Implementing, and Assessing Lessons

I can't believe a child actually made this book!

—Melissa, Grade 1
(about her own book)

Students participating in Artists/Writers Workshop often create finished pieces that are quite stunning. Because the results are so impressive, it is easy for teachers to become focused on completing the project or creating the finished product. Especially with the school day packed with mandated curriculum, it is easy to lose sight of the rich, dynamic literary (and literacy) process students can be engaged in to reach that end. When the focus becomes creating the finished product, it is tempting to cut corners to save time in order to complete the project more quickly.

But I caution teachers against concentrating on the finished product rather than on making the most of the rich literacy learning made available to students throughout the process. Students' published pieces should serve as testimony to the depth of their learning and the rich process they have been engaged in.

Likewise, those who see this as an occasional activity, such as once a week on Friday afternoons, are missing the point. Artists/Writers Workshop is meant to be facilitated as an ongoing *process*. It is not intended to be viewed as a special project or used as a reward at the end of a busy week. Although it certainly can be treated in that manner, that choice deprives students of the full benefits they would reap from participating in this dynamic pathway into literacy learning as part of their regular writing process in the classroom.

While ideally Artists/Writers Workshop would occur daily, in today's curriculum-heavy schools this may not be possible—and it isn't essential. The research findings outlined in Appendix A, which document significant gains in reading and writing skills (particularly for students at risk), were the result of implementing Artists/Writers Workshop three times a week for sixty to seventy-five minutes per session. If this kind of time segment seems unrealistic given your daily schedule, Artists/Writers Workshop may be facilitated in smaller blocks of time throughout the week. Keep in mind that the process I'm describing is a dynamic vehicle for teachers to teach students what they need to learn—in a way that reaches all students, not just the verbal learners. This rich process is well worth the time it takes; it can be the very means for teaching required curriculum effectively to *all* students—and not just something else to squeeze into the day. Keep in mind that Artists/Writers Workshop epitomizes what Renate and Geoffrey Caine (1994) describe as "orchestrated immersion," which is one of the key components of effective teaching and learning.

Units of Study

I have found the Artists/Writers Workshop approach to be most effective when organized around ongoing units of study. Particularly when genre studies are integrated into the science or social studies curriculum, it allows a class to build community word banks around a common theme as well as share acquired knowledge of the topic under study.

Integration with the science or social studies curriculum (or both) also helps with time management issues. Addressing two areas of the curriculum—language arts and science, for instance—frees up more time for the art-making part of the process, which naturally is going to take a bit longer than a straight writing workshop. It is also important to keep in mind quality over quantity.

Either process I describe in this book, crayon-resist or collage, can be used to develop units of study in science or social studies. Over the years, I have developed several Picturing Writing crayon-resist integrated units of study that can serve as models for the integration of many other curriculum themes. These foundational units include a time-of-day descriptive writing unit (which I consider to be the best and simplest introduction to the process), weather poetry, a winter story unit, and an animals in their habitat research-based story unit. I have also developed several Image-Making (collage) units of study: the original Image-Making Within The Writing Process in which students discover stories in their individual portfolios of hand-painted papers, an Image-Making integrated curriculum poetry unit (which integrates well with many science and social studies themes), and a research-based story unit on endangered species (which also can be used as a model for research-based stories on a number of topics).

Once you begin to explore the Artists/Writers Workshop process, you will be able to determine which of your curriculum themes adapt well to this approach. Most topics that take place in the natural world are a good bet. Studies of various biomes, animals within those biomes, landforms, plant life, life cycles, trees through the seasons—anything you can *picture* will generally lend itself to this visual approach to writing. Dry science topics such as magnets or machines (I hope I have not offended anyone) or social studies topics such as government are not particularly suited to this visual approach. As a general rule, if it is a visual topic—something that can be *seen* in nature—it is likely to be a good fit.

I have also dabbled in straight report writing using this approach. Fourth-grade students created stunning animal reports, with each student choosing a favorite New Hampshire animal to study. Their teacher helped them identify several topics to research within their study (habitat, physical characteristics, prey, predators, other interesting facts) and each topic of their investigation became a page in their book that was also supported by a crayon resist painting based on the information they had gleaned. Once again, the pictures preceded the writing. For student examples of how Artists/Writers Workshop can be tailored to address both a particular genre and a thematic unit within the curriculum, visit www.picturingwriting.org/studentwork.html.

Planning a Unit

Once you have gotten a feel for the rhythm and flow of Artists/Writers Workshop by watching the accompanying DVD and experimenting with the process via the introductory mini-lessons contained in this book, I hope you will consider further exploration. Until you and your students have developed some level of comfort and expertise with the process, I suggest you keep your sights modest. A single piece of art and writing or a series of individual pieces (either descriptive passages or poetry) around a common theme will allow you the flexibility of moving on when you and your students are ready. (Once you become involved in a story unit, which is far more complex and sophisticated in its scope, you are committed to moving through all the story parts. This will be a much lengthier process and should be undertaken only once you and your students have completed a few simpler units of study.) To undertake more complex units of study, I highly recommend participating in experiential teacher training.

Whenever I plan a unit of study, I like to use the process of back planning. First I identify a theme within the curriculum that I would like to design my unit around. Then I consider the Language Arts standards for the particular grade level. I also decide what shape this writing project will take: Do I want to begin with writing descriptive passages so I can support students in building a foundation of descriptive vocabulary? Do I want to focus on developing a sense of setting? Would I prefer to use poetry as a vehicle for expanding vocabulary and exploring word use? Are my students ready for a story unit? Or a unit that combines research with developing a research-based story? I envision what I want the final product to look like. Then I start planning backward—thinking about the process. What skills do my students need to successfully complete this unit of study? What mini-lessons do I need to offer to support the development of those skills? I create a list of skills necessary to the project. Which of those skills will be a matter of review and which will be new to my students?

Figure 7.1 presents a unit of study planning sheet. Once I list the skills that need to be either reviewed or introduced, I begin to think about the literature I have available to use during my mini-lessons. For instance, in the mini-lessons in Chapter Nine, writing a descriptive passage is the

---

Artists/Writers Workshop
Integrated Curriculum Unit Planner

Theme:

Art Medium:

Type(s) of writing:

Vision of final product:

Art skills to review:

Art skills to introduce:

Writing skills to review:

Writing skills to introduce:

Resources available   Uses
_____   _____

Figure 7.1.   Unit planning worksheet.

ultimate goal. I have selected Ralph Fletcher's *Twilight Comes Twice* for the Literature Share because I love Ralph's use of descriptive language, and in particular, his use of personification.

As modeled in the DVD, my mini-lesson will focus on painting pictures with words through the use of personification.

I also understand that I am going to be introducing both art and writing skills so I look for picture books that will help me to introduce basic (art or literary) concepts that suit my lessons. The time of day sample lessons (Chapter Nine) begin with painting the sky, considering the colors of the sky at different times of day, introducing crayon resist and interesting ground-lines, and modeling how to make tissue clouds. I look through picture books to find pictures that will help me introduce those basic concepts.

Once I have identified the literature I will use, I also try to organize my mini-lessons in a logical sequence, moving from simple to more complex. What are the very first skills my students will need in order to be successful? Once they have acquired those skills, what skills will I introduce next? Part of my planning process involves my belief that students are most successful in any new endeavor if they are given the tools they need when they need them. I envision the students' process and organize my lessons accordingly.

As I develop a new unit of study, I like to keep a notebook of what I did each day, what worked and what didn't. While I know this note-keeping can be one more thing to do in an already way-too-busy day, when you want to implement the project next year you will be grateful for your notes.

Facilitating the Process

Once you have completed the planning phase of designing a new unit of study, it will be important to review the basic Artists/Writers Workshop format, which involves the following four steps in each daily lesson:

+ Literature Share/Discussion
+ Modeling Session
+ Work Session
+ Group Share

As you facilitate Artists/Writers Workshop following this simple four-step format, keep in mind that you will be teaching in two languages—through pictures and through words. In fact, it can be helpful to think about delivering mini-lessons in two complementary strands as modeled in the DVD: one that addresses the language of pictures and the other addresses the language of words. A single Artists/Writers Workshop would typically include these four activities, often focusing either on one language or the other. However, I always keep in mind that the ultimate goal is the marriage of pictures and words: how the two languages work together to tell the whole story.

Rhythm and Flow

Beyond mapping out the two strands of mini-lessons (for creating pictures and for writing words), you also need to decide ahead of time whether or not to have your students develop an entire picture sequence first (supported by literature-based mini-lessons) and then go back to write to each picture (again supported by literature-based mini-lessons). Alternatively, you can ask students to "paint and write, paint and write." In the latter case, your unit will weave back and forth between mini-lessons that address the language of pictures and the language of words. Note that whichever method you choose, the art always precedes the writing.

Each approach has advantages and disadvantages. Very young children, English language learners, or other students without strong verbal skills often find it helpful to anchor an entire story idea (if indeed you are developing stories) in pictures first before tackling the writing. (Here they have a chance to use their strengths to develop and record their ideas before they venture into the writing, which is apt to be a more challenging arena for them.) On the other hand, a "paint and write, paint and write" rhythm breaks up the writing, interspersing it with painting and retaining the interest of students who need more activity. If you opt for having your students complete their picture sequence before starting the writing, make sure your students have regular opportunities to orally rehearse their pictures as they move through the picture drafting process and before they write.

Single pieces of art and writing clearly warrant a "paint and write" approach.

Step by Step

The following sections provide a deeper look at the factors to consider at each stage of the workshop process. These factors require attention whichever rhythm you decide to establish in your classroom and whether you are facilitating an art mini-lesson or a writing mini-lesson.

Literature Share/Discussion

Begin Artists/Writers Workshop by sharing a piece of quality literature selected for a particular purpose. Whether the focus of the day centers on studying the language of pictures or the language of words (or how the two work together to tell the whole story), find a picture book that both exemplifies the type of craft you care to focus on and addresses the theme of your unit of study in a grade-appropriate way. Depending on the specific purpose of your mini-lesson, you may choose to read an entire picture book or to share excerpts or discuss illustrations only.

By defining your students as artists and writers (not as *author-illustrators,* as mentioned in Chapter Two), you prime them to view picture books from an insider's perspective. They are eager to learn from the masters and thus from the mentor texts you present, scouring them for guiding principles of either an artistic or literary nature. Their level of engagement and the deep understanding they develop through this visual approach to literacy learning can be extraordinary. By processing information in two languages (the language of words and the language of pictures), students broaden their grasp of key literary elements and art concepts and how the two complement each other.

Students are also inspired to apply these understandings to their own work. Second grader Chelsea explains, "You look at books and you say hey, I want to try this. I want to make a picture like that." Jared proudly remarks, "I think my book came out as good as the book that I was reading."

Modeling Session

A Modeling Session follows the Literature Share/Discussion. This is a teacher-facilitated activity in which students participate as a whole group in the very task they will soon be undertaking on their own. That is, within the context of creating a class piece, you walk students, step by step, through the entire art and writing process, one lesson at a time. Whether modeling creating a piece of art or a piece of writing, each Modeling Session has a clear literary purpose.

While you are modeling, plan on asking a series of questions that invite students to direct the outcome (at least in part). To accomplish this successfully, you will need a clear understanding of what your specific objectives are for that particular modeling session. Then, within that framework, invite your students to offer suggestions. As you receive their responses to your questions, you will appreciate them all and only use those that further the ultimate objectives of the lesson. The resulting piece (of art or writing) is truly a "class piece," the result of weaving together several students' ideas guided by your own teaching objectives.

During each Modeling Session, I try to apply new understandings gleaned from the literature studies as well as to reinforce previously introduced skills and concepts in art or in writing as students respond to the questions I pose. By eliciting suggestions and direction from students, I actively engage the class in the creative process. Students develop a sense of ownership over the resulting piece that keeps them engaged and prepares them to jump into the driver's seat during their subsequent Work Session.

Whether the unit of study involves crafting a series of single pieces of art and descriptive writing or poems, or developing an entire story in pictures and in words over several weeks, the goal during each session is to offer explicit teacher-facilitated, student-directed modeling of the immediate task at hand. Students participate in a dry run as a whole class before diving into their individual work.

Work Session

The Work Session is the time when students apply their ever-growing pool of knowledge about art, writing, and the topic of the unit of study to their own work. Their study of quality picture books and your modeling of the process infuse the Work Session with an understanding of new concepts and a clear sense of purpose and process. Students enter their art or writing process with intention.

A Work Session is most productive when it follows immediately after the Modeling Session, while vision and sense of purpose are fresh in students' minds. It should last roughly thirty to forty-five minutes (with the entire workshop lasting between sixty and ninety minutes for all four steps). If there is not time to have the Work Session follow directly after the Modeling Session, a quick review will help remind students of the immediate task at hand before they dive in.

During a Work Session, I like to play relaxing music to create an ambiance conducive to focused attention and creative thinking. If students are writing, I ask them to place their piece of art in a desktop easel stand so they can better view their work. (I discuss desktop easels in more depth in Appendix B.) As with Literature Shares and Modeling Sessions, it is useful to hold a Work Session at least two or three times a week, to give your students time to apply the skills they are learning. Students engaged in this process benefit from the sustained sense of continuity that comes from having the opportunity to return regularly to their work-in-progress. If they have only occasional and sporadic opportunities to revisit their work, students find it harder to sustain a sense of flow and connection from one mini-lesson to the next. This is particularly true when students are working on a story.

While you may think of this time as a *work* session, your students probably won't. I remember one rainy spring day when Linda Ball's second graders were working on their Picturing Writing research-based animal stories (during which time the cover of this book was created by Logan). When Linda announced that in five minutes it would be time to stop writing and go to lunch, a group moan echoed across the room. At that cue, Linda proceeded to assure the class, "But the good news is that it is raining out today so we will be having indoor recess. After lunch you can come directly back to the classroom to continue work-ing on your stories." Her students burst into a spontaneous round of applause.

Group Share

At the end of each Work Session, invite a few students to share their work. They place their artwork in an Artists Frame (as described in Chapter Six and in Appendix B and modeled in the DVD), a device that serves to honor the piece by literally framing it as well as drawing students' attention to the work.

Young artists and writers (particularly first graders!) are very eager to share. It is a good idea to establish a system that ensures that all students who want to share will get a turn before a classmate has a chance to share again. Without such a system, you're likely to be bombarded regularly by a chorus of "Can I share? Can I share?" To avoid this, I keep a class list on a clipboard or taped to the back of the

Artists Frame. Every time a student shares, I jot down the date beside that child's name. Sometimes, beside the date, I write an "A" for art or a "W" for writing. That way I maintain a running record of not only who has shared and who hasn't, but also who has shared their art and who has shared their writing. I make sure students understand that everyone will have a turn to share before we begin a second round of sharing. This seems to satisfy those who want to share every day and puts an end to the predictable chorus of requests.

When you're working with older students, eagerness to share may not be an issue. I still like to maintain a record of who has shared, even with older students, to make sure I offer all students the opportunity to share their work.

Selecting Students to Share   To maximize the potential of the Group Share as a teaching tool, I select pieces of art or writing each day based on the following criteria, in this order:

1. The student's work reflects the application of a concept we have recently discussed.
2. The student has made a noticeable leap in art or writing.
3. The student is having a bad day and could benefit from some positive feedback.
4. The student has not had a chance to share yet.

My selection of whom to invite to share is usually purposeful.

How Group Share Works   Even if the purpose of the Group Share will be to focus on the writing, writing is always viewed in relation to the picture from which it was crafted. As described in Chapter Six and Appendix B, the student who is sharing sits in the Artists/Writers Chair, which is placed at the back of the circle opposite the Artists Frame, so the artist is able to see the art from the same perspective as the group.

I like to begin the Artists Share with an open-ended invitation: "Tell us what you were thinking when you created your piece." This makes room for students to discuss their thought process in a non-directed fashion. Sometimes young students or students who lack strong verbal skills have a difficult time responding to such an open-ended invitation and may need a bit more coaxing. Then I will ask more specific, directed questions (depending on the theme of their picture). With an introductory time of day painting, for example, I would ask the student to tell what time of day the painting shows and to describe the visual signs of that in the picture. ("How did you show that?" invites recognition of important details.) I am always looking for ways to encourage students to share what they were thinking as they created their piece. This will also become easier with practice as students learn to be more reflective throughout their work session.

Then, depending on your instructional objectives for the Group Share (and what you have planned next for your students), you may choose one or more of the following directions:

✦   Reinforce certain skills by drawing students' attention to specific aspects of the picture. ("I notice that Devyn remembered to create an interesting ground-line and that he thought about reflection when he painted his pond the same color as the sky.") You see me do this on the DVD.

✦   Pursue a series of purposeful questions. ("Tyler, could you tell us what time of day it is in your picture?") You can also ask for information about the weather, the season, the place depicted, thus prepping students to develop a sense of setting in their writing.

✦   Ask the "doing question." ("Can you tell us what your sun is doing?") Generally, I ask this question in order to elicit strong verbs. On the DVD you will see this question elicit some very rich language. If appropriate to your goals, you can create a list of "doing words" offered by students for a particular object being discussed (as explained in more detail later in this section).

✦   Invite the artist to call on a few friends for comments or questions.

Students of all ages can be taught how to offer constructive feedback or ask thoughtful questions. When students have something positive to say, they can begin their comment with "I like . . . " and continue with a specific observation. Rather than just saying, "I like your picture," I encourage students to tell *exactly* what they like about the picture. This fosters development of a keener aesthetic eye.

If students do not have something positive to say, they may either remain silent or frame their comment as a question. Perhaps a classmate is confused by something in the picture. A question might begin with "I wonder": "I wonder why you painted your sky green. What time of day is it supposed to be?" Sometimes questions can be posed truly out of curiosity: "I like the way your trees look. I wonder how you made that texture on your trees?" Of course, once students get in the habit of offering positive comments or asking questions, they need not be limited to those precise ways of commenting or asking questions. I offer those suggestions to students at the beginning of the year as a way to launch and maintain a constructive Group Share.

I like to wrap up an individual share with a positive comment—again either reinforcing a skill already introduced ("I notice that Sarah was careful to wash her brush so as to keep her colors from getting muddy") or emphasizing a new insight ("I notice that Michael did something we have not yet discussed. Look at the sense of depth he has created in his picture. Notice how some objects look close up and some look far away. Michael, can you tell us how you accomplished that?" and then: "Perhaps some of you would like to try that.")

After two or three students have had a chance to talk about their work (and this should not go on too long or the group may become restless), I like to wrap up the Group Share with a concluding observation to the group such as, "Did you notice how unique and different everyone's art work is? That is one of the wonderful things about doing art" or "I can tell people are really making thoughtful decisions about their artwork and applying many of the concepts we have seen professional illustrators use."

Sometimes I use the end of an art share to brainstorm silver dollar words that I think will be useful in the upcoming writing session. For instance, if students will be writing about winter paintings, I will ask students what the snow in the picture in the Artists Frame is doing. (There is that "doing question" again.) If students tell me the snow is coming down, I ask for silver dollar ways to say that. We then begin the brainstorming process. As I call on students, I create a class word bank for Snow, which I will later post on the wall or type up, copy, and hand out to keep in their writing folders or ever-expanding class-generated thesauruses. The list is likely to include words such as *drifting, blowing, sprinkling, swirling, twirling, whirling, falling, falling softly, gently, lightly, silently.* (Notice that if students tell me the snow is falling, I can ask them how the snow is falling and thereby elicit a list of adverbs.)

While a writing share follows the same format, the discussion may focus on the language of words (by themselves) or how they work with the picture. Students may observe that the writer's words indeed paint a picture or that the words, when viewed with the picture, create an illusion of movement ("make the picture come alive"). Like the artists share, the depth of the conversation will vary with the grade level. I often steer the conversation to analyzing just what a particular student did to create such a successful piece. Thus we get to practice, once again, reading like a writer.

If a piece of writing or art leaves something to be desired and I feel inclined to offer suggestions, I will always sandwich my suggestion in between two positive comments.

> Kara, I notice that you included a few nice strong adjectives in your writing. That really helps to paint a picture in my mind. I am wondering if you want to revisit your writing in order to strengthen your verbs. That might really enhance your writing and help bring your picture to life. Let's see if you can make some magic with your words. You are almost there.

Of course, like any teacher, I tailor my comments to the individual student. If an emergent writer or nonverbal student has included *one* strong verb in their writing, I am delighted. I am going to focus on that rather than focus on all the weaker words that could stand improvement. I will, however, encourage more capable students to continue to refine their work.

Happy Accidents and Learning Experiences Within Artists/Writers Workshop we often talk about "happy accidents" and "learning experiences." A happy accident is something unexpected that happens while we are creating a picture. It is a surprise, but a pleasant one. We are pleased with the results. The happy accidents that punctuate our creative endeavors are part of the fun of doing art. A happy accident, shared with others, might encourage classmates to try for a similar effect. (In the DVD, you will hear students talking about happy accidents.)

A learning experience is also something unexpected that happens while we are creating a picture. We are not so pleased with the result *but we can learn from the experience* and because of that, it is a valuable experience and worthy of sharing with fellow artists. Perhaps I wet my paper too much when creating a watercolor wash and then proceeded to brush the paper with paint over and over again until the paper became all mealy and eventually tore. This offers a valuable lesson learned and sharing it will benefit classmates so they can avoid the same fate.

Or perhaps I created an interesting ground-line with crayon and then proceeded to draw a tree in front of it. The ground-line now appears to go right through the center of my tree trunk, cutting my tree in half. I am not happy with the result but I can learn from this experience. I can also share this "learning experience" with my classmates and thus spare them the same experience.

Learning experiences often trigger creative problem solving and are valuable in that regard as well. Perhaps, with the help of classmates, I can figure out how to rescue my picture. Or perhaps I will decide to redo my picture, having figured out how to avoid the same fate in the future. Learning experience can help build a sense of community (artists learning from each other) and can also trigger discussions about revision.

Share Regularly Since the Group Share falls at the end of the Work Session, it is often tempting to skip it because some students are still happily engaged in their work and only five or ten minutes remain before it is time to move on to the next activity—or you have actually run out of time before you notice, which is easy to do, since a classroom full of students engaged in their work is tempting to allow to continue.

While I confess that I too have chosen to skip the Group Share on occasion, I advise you not to make this a common practice. Without the Group Share, students miss the opportunity for community building, as well as opportunities to reinforce skills and learn from each other. Because Artists/Writers Workshop is greatly enriched by inviting students to share their work and their experiences, if you don't have time to hold a Group Share at the end of the Work Session, find another time later that day or the next day to hold your Group Share. You won't regret it.

Thinking in Complementary Strands

As an example of cycling through Artists/Writers Workshop in two strands, suppose I want to teach how to develop a sense of setting in pictures and in words. First, I gather books that contain various pictures of settings to share with my students. As a part of the Literature Share, we analyze what visual elements illustrators include in their "setting pictures" as well as what art concepts might be applied. For example, students might notice that a setting picture includes information about the time of day, the weather, the season (sometimes), and the place. They may also notice that the illustrator chooses to use a long distance view (rather than a close-up) to show more information about the place. We may observe that in order to create a sense of depth in the setting picture, the illustrator made objects in the foreground bigger and objects in the background smaller. This brief analysis of a setting picture and discussion about one or more basic art concepts can be repeated while looking at several different setting pictures. Students will start to observe patterns in the way illustrators establish a sense of setting in their pictures.

I then model creating a setting picture using the same medium that I will make available to my students. During the Modeling Session, I try to apply some of the concepts or understandings just articulated during the Literature Share. Then, during the subsequent Work Session, students create their own setting pictures, applying some of those new understandings as well as skills previously introduced. During the Group Share, we discuss some of their work, commenting on applications of the concepts we have been discussing.

In the next mini-lesson (on a different day), during the Literature Share I address the element of setting from the verbal perspective by looking at how authors establish a sense of setting by crafting their words. We would analyze what kinds of information the author includes in the description of the setting (parallel to analyzing what kinds of information the illustrator includes in the setting picture). Depending on the grade level, we would analyze one or more leads for setting information and most likely discover that to establish a sense of setting, the author includes information about time of day, weather, season, and place. (Note that this runs parallel to the information offered in the setting picture.)

Following that discussion, I model—with the students' help—how to craft a quality lead sentence, applying what the class observed during our literature study. During the Work Session, students craft their own leads, a few of which will be shared during the Group Share. Lead sentences are always viewed in relation to the "lead picture," which is placed in the Artists Frame. Moving through the Artists/Writers Workshop format in this way, in two complementary strands (an art strand and a writing strand), is modeled during the Artists/Writers Workshop Overview in the companion DVD.

While it might seem like a lot of additional work to teach two sets of lessons, using two languages for the same topic, that effort to teach using two languages is what makes the difference between reaching the whole class and losing those who are not verbal learners. When you try this process and see for yourself how enthusiastic, engaged, and successful *all your students* become, the "extra work" will be well worth the effort. Personally, I find the rewards of seeing the "low performers" succeed makes it well worth the time. And don't overlook that fact that this approach will also push your midrange and top students to grow in new and interesting ways.

How Planning and Implementation Guide Assessment

Developing your own integrated curriculum units of study (large or small), to be facilitated within Artists/Writers Workshop, requires some thought as to the scope and sequence of lessons you will want to present. You would have identified a theme within your curriculum, and if there is a curriculum framework, you would have reviewed it. Perhaps you even reviewed your state standards in language arts for your grade level. If you are an art specialist, you may have reviewed your state's curriculum frameworks in visual arts. Whether or not you went through this sort of rigor, you have an intuitive sense of what skills are expected of your students at your grade level. The worksheet depicted in Figure 7.1 may be helpful to you in thinking through and developing your unit of study.

Participating in a planning process such as this will help you to identify skills in both art and writing that you would like to either review or introduce. You also have envisioned the final form of your unit of study or end result. Through the process of back planning, you develop a sequence of mini-lessons based on ordering these objectives in some sort of logical order.

Of course, we all learn from our experiences. Figure 7.2 offers a form that may be used as a daily record of the mini-lessons units of study you devise. I suggest enlarging this form and making multiple copies to keep in a three-ring binder. As you facilitate Artists/Writers Workshop from day to day, maintain a record of what you did, what worked well, and how you would improve upon the lesson next year. While this may seem like one more thing you don't have time for, you will be grateful next year when your memory evades you.

As you enter the Artists/Writers Workshop process, you are clear about your teaching objectives—whether it be for each art mini-lesson or each writing mini-lesson. You keep these objectives "in the back of your mind" as you analyze picture books and model the art and writing process using available resources. This includes but is not limited to using picture books as mentor texts. You may even devise a checklist of expectations for your students: items you hope they will include or consider in their art and in their writing based on the Literature Share/Discussions and the Modeling Sessions. These checklists will vary greatly, of course, depending on the unit and on the grade level this.

During the introductory time-of-day study that is launched by the mini-lessons outlined in Chapter Nine and modeled on the DVD, your checklist for students for the art portion of their work may look like this

Did you:

+ Create an interesting ground-line?
+ Include information about the time of day?
+ Show reflection of the sky on the water? (optional)
+ Include tissue clouds? (optional)
+ Keep your colors from getting muddy?
+ Fill in all your white spaces?

The checklist for the writing portion of the project, which focuses on establishing a sense of setting and mood in a piece of writing, may look like the one in the second box.

Artists/Writers Workshop
Daily Record

Theme:

Date:

Lesson objective:

Focus: (art or writing)

Skills introduced:

Skills Reviewed:

Book(s):

Literature Share/Discussion:

Modeling:

Work Session:

Group Share:

Comment:

Figure 7.2.   Daily mini-lesson recording sheet.

Did you:

+ Tell about the time of day?
+ Tell about the place?
+ Use silver dollar
  • adjectives?
  • verbs?
  • adverbs?
+ Did you include any personification?
+ Did you include any alliteration?
+ Did you read over your paragraph to see if your words paint a picture of your painting?
+ Did you create strong mood in your writing?
+ Did you check over your writing to see if it
  • makes sense?
  • uses correct spelling?
  • uses correct punctuation?
  • has maintained consistent verb tense?
  • has maintained subject-verb agreement?

Of course, the checklist for your students would be tailored to your grade level expectations. The lists I have suggested here would be appropriate for the third-grade classroom you see in the DVD, a group that is fairly new to the process.

As you develop more research-based integrated curriculum units, you might add an item to each of your checklists that asks students to embed factual information in their work (art and writing, as appropriate). You will be surprised how much content information can be embedded in a piece of art, and once considered within the art, can be easily embedded in the writing.

Checklists such as these not only serve to remind students what to include in their initial work or what to consider during the revision process, they can also be used to evaluate your students' art and writing. It makes sense that the same checklist developed for your students can be used to evaluate whether or not your students are following through applying these skills and concepts that were introduced or reinforced in the mini-lessons to their own work (art or writing).

There is an additional benefit to developing a set of checklists. When I use this more consciously planned approach to the development and teaching of a unit of study and the mini-lessons within it, I become clearer about my objectives. I find it easier to embed those objectives in my Literature Shares/Discussions, Modeling Sessions, and Group Shares, and I can offer my students clear verbal reminders, checklists on the board, or paper checklists that clearly articulate the objectives for a particular art or writing experience. Checklists also provide students (and teachers) with a basis for evaluating their work. By revisiting the checklists I have created for my students, I will basically be evaluating whether or not they have applied the skills (art and writing) that I have taught.

While most classroom teachers are accustomed to evaluating writing, unless they are art specialists or have a background in art, they are not accustomed to evaluating art. While a particular painting or piece of art may be more or less pleasing to me, but I generally try to evaluate artwork based on the student's attempts to apply the skills I have taught. Some students clearly begin the process with stronger visual acuity and the ability to represent the natural world using art materials than others. Knowing this, I try to focus on whether or not each student has met most or all of my objectives. And as always, in the back of my mind, I am following the student's growth as an artist and conveyer of visual information. Some criteria for this are laid out in Chapters Eight and Nine.

As teachers we are all held accountable for our students' learning. Student assessment can also serve as a personal barometer for teachers, indicating whether or not we have met our own objectives for the class. If my students have not been able to follow through applying the concepts or skills I have introduced or reinforced during my mini-lessons, I need to look at my own teaching practice. Perhaps I should offer a review as *I* clearly have not done an adequate job. That said, you will be amazed at how much learning actually occurs—particularly among your "low-performing students"—when concepts and skills are introduced using these visual tools and reinforced throughout the process.

Self-Assessment

Through a guided self-assessment process, students can learn how to look at and improve their own work. They learn to reflect on their work and their process as well as naturally begin to internalize the criteria for evaluating their work. Reflective practice such as this can be embedded in the Group Share, revision, self-assessment activities, and their writing an About the Artist/Writer page to be included at the back of the published piece. I always like to read students' thoughtful comments on their author pages such as the one second-grade Chelsea wrote: "My story inspired me with all of my hard work and my dream came true. It was almost done! I think my book is magnificent because I worked so hard!" or Jared's: "I think my book came out as good as the book that I was reading."

8 Developing Visual Literacy

Study of Two Picture Books

You look at books and you say hey, I want to try this.
I want to make a picture like that.

—Chelsea, Grade 2

In *Ways of Telling: Conversations on the Art of the Picture Book,* Leonard Marcus writes, "A picture book is a dialogue between two worlds: the world of images and the world of words" (2002, p. 3). That dialogue, and in fact marriage of two worlds—the interweaving of the language of pictures and the language of words—communicates more than either language alone could ever convey. The expression "the whole is greater than the sum of its parts" takes on new meaning as you consider how the words of a picture book enhance the pictures and how the pictures enhance the words. Together they offer an expression far greater than each alone.

During Artists/Writers Workshop, students become immersed in the study of quality picture books. You will soon discover that the very same picture books that have been sitting on your classroom shelves for years offer a wealth of examples of the artful marriage between pictures and words, and the key to literacy learning for some of your most reluctant learners. You may suddenly feel like you have discovered a hidden treasure chest in your very own classroom. And the truth is, you may well have.

Of course, not all picture books are equal. To determine which picture books will best serve your instructional purposes, I encourage you to do several quick "book walks." While it is more typical to analyze the text of a picture book for its literary elements, this time focus on the pictures, particularly those that tell about the setting, who the characters are, what the problem is, what the solution is, and what happens at the end of the story. As you read the pictures, you will discover that in quality picture books, these key literary elements are expressed through pictures as well as words. A whole new world of teaching possibilities has just opened up to you! As you prepare to use your picture books as mentor texts, you may find yourself embarking on your own journey of discovery.

This chapter provides examples of how you and your students might look at visual elements within selected picture books to develop an understanding of the craft of meaning-making through the language of pictures and the language of words. For simplicity, when I refer to *readers,* I mean those absorbing the words of the story, whether by eye or by ear, who "hear" its words, either with their physical ears or their mental ones.

After walking through *Owl Moon* by Jane Yolen (illustrated by John Schoenherr) in some detail, I turn to *Wild Horse Winter,* written and illustrated by Tetsuya Honda, to offer further insights. I then show how Jared, a second grader, makes use of these concepts to construct a picture book of his own.

Owl Moon: The Seamless Dance of Pictures and Words

Owl Moon (1987), written by Jane Yolen and illustrated by John Schoenherr, offers many excellent examples of how the marriage of words and pictures work together to tell a whole story. Before even turning to the first page of the story, you can see how the language of pictures plays a critical role in the front matter of this Caldecott Award–winning book. On the cover, the title page, and the dedication page, pictures and words work together to prepare the reader to enter the story.

Cover Picture and Title

The cover picture and the title of *Owl Moon* work together to convey important information to prospective readers (Figure 8.1). Hiding the cover picture makes it clear that while the title alone is intriguing, it provides no information about who the characters are or where the story takes place. We can only guess at the meaning of "Owl Moon." Conversely, with the title hidden, the cover picture introduces the characters and the setting (place, time of day, weather, and season), but doesn't begin to suggest that an owl is central to the story. These two elements, the cover picture and the title, work in partnership to tell the reader what the story is about.

Figure 8.1.   Cover of *Owl Moon*.

The cover picture also serves to invite the reader into the story. With your eye drawn to the bright circle of the full moon, you cannot help but notice the two characters positioned directly in front of the moon. A father extends his arm to the young child, encouraging the child as they tromp through the snow on this winter's night. The positioning of the characters and their body language also serve as an invitation to the reader. The child's body language—arm outstretched toward the father, leg lifted in mid-stride and scarf blowing behind—suggests motion and an eagerness to accept that invitation. The moonlight reflecting on the snow-covered hills also serves to invite the reader into what otherwise might feel like a rather cold and uninviting place. Clearly the moon will light our way. The prospective reader wants to go along too, wondering where the two are going and why this book is called *Owl Moon*. Notice how the bare trees frame the moon and the characters, providing a presence and a sense of mystery that becomes further accentuated later in the story.

Title Page

More and more picture books have a picture of some sort on the inside title page. On the title page of *Owl Moon* (Figure 8.2), the reader finds the young child, all bundled up in snowsuit, hat, mittens, and boots, standing in an open doorway looking out into the winter's night. The image suggests that the child has just added a scarf, one end of it still in mid-air. This image provides a visual invitation to the reader to join the child in stepping into the vastness of the winter night. With the open doorway leading into the deep blue night in stark contrast to the empty white page (containing only print), the eye is drawn outward, which serves to create a sense of the reader being drawn outside as well. This picture of the young child at the doorway also hints at what we later discover: that the story is told through the eyes of that child.

Dedication Page

The next page, the dedication page, shows an owl soaring overhead; a shadow of that owl is depicted below. Though the rest of the page is blank except for the dedication itself, the owl's direction and implied

Figure 8.2.   Title page.

motion leads the reader directly into the story. This visual hook provides further incentive to turn the page, while the shadow serves as a reminder that the moon is full on this particular night, all the better for spotting owls. . . . This small visual touch on the dedication page also foreshadows what is to come. We see the owl heading right into the book. Through thoughtful attention to the visual handling of the front matter, John Schoenherr artfully draws readers into the book before they even arrive at the first page of the story.

Note that the two dedications connect the author and the illustrator to the adventure that is about to take place. Jane Yolen writes, "For my husband David, who took all of our children owling." Illustrator John

Schoenherr writes, "For my granddaughter, Nyssa, for when she is old enough to go owling." Students can be encouraged to create dedications that are in some way connected to the meaning of their story. They can also be encouraged to include some sort of small picture on the dedication page that connects the reader to the story.

Setting Picture

On his very first illustration (which I also refer to as the "lead picture" because its function parallels that of the lead sentences), Schoenherr pulls the reader way back, using a long-distance perspective as he sets the stage for the story (Figure 8.3). This is no accident. To establish a strong sense of setting, the artist wants the reader to step back and see the big picture—metaphorically as well as literally—so Schoenherr chooses to depict the opening scene from a long-distance perspective. This enables him to show much more of the place than he could with a mid-range view or a close-up. Not only does Schoenherr show the big picture, he chooses to depict the setting from an unusual perspective— from above, as if seen by someone flying overhead. An owl, perhaps?

Establishing Mood

Schoenherr skillfully establishes the mood on the very first picture through his use of color and texture (or more specifically, the lack thereof). The overall mood of the picture is quiet and calm, supported by his use of muted blue tones and the lack of texture. Though the sky is white, the nighttime setting is made clear from the combination of the cool tones, the limited color palette, almost all consisting of shades of blue, and the long shadows cast by the moon. (Though the moon is not in view, its presence is suggested by the quality and color of the shadows.) Despite the lack of sun or moon in the picture, the reader understands that it is night.

Reading Setting Information

It is easy to read this picture for what I refer to as "setting information": *What time of day is it? What kind of day is it (weather and mood)? What season is it? Where does the story take place?* As students respond to these

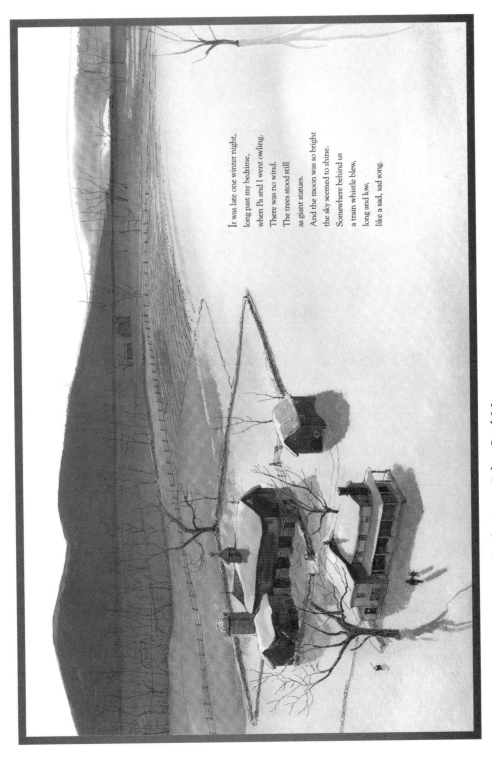

It was late one winter night,
long past my bedtime,
when Pa and I went owling.
There was no wind.
The trees stood still
as giant statues.
And the moon was so bright
the sky seemed to shine.
Somewhere behind us
a train whistle blew,
long and low,
like a sad, sad song.

Figure 8.3.   Setting or "lead picture" for *Owl Moon*.

questions as they read the picture for setting information, follow each piece of information the students provide by asking one simple question: *How do you know that?*

Asking students to articulate the particulars—what visual details they observe that provide them with specific setting information—serves to enhance students' ability to read pictures for meaning and to link this meaning to the visual information provided. For instance, if a student looking at this first illustration in *Owl Moon* were to tell me that it is night, I would ask, *"How do you know that?"* I expect that student (or classmates) to provide me with specific visual details that inform the reader that it is night. A student might tell me that the area of sky around the train (in the upper right of the page) is dark, or that the mountains are dark, or that the quality of the shadows that appear on the snow suggest that there is a full moon. While shadows could appear in a daytime picture, the cool muted blue tones of the picture convey the quiet and dim lighting of night.

Creating a Sense of Depth

Notice how Schoenherr establishes the vastness of the place in his setting picture by creating a sense of depth through the thoughtful depiction of the size of objects as well as the intensity of color in the foreground, the mid-ground, and the background. Notice that the objects in the foreground are bigger and so appear closer to the viewer. They also have more color and more detail. Notice the large, detailed colored barns in the foreground in contrast to the faint, very small muted house, barn, and silo way in the distance, which have very little color or detail. This is a clear example of how objects designed to look relatively nearby are larger, brighter, and more detailed; objects intended to appear more distant are smaller, more muted, and have less detail. As outlined in the gray box, these basic understandings can be applied by students to create a sense of depth in their pictures.

Notice the size of the trees in the foreground, the mid-ground, and the background. The trees in the foreground are larger than those in the mid-ground and background. They also have more texture (detail) on them. The trees in the distance are smaller and have no texture and less detail. They also lack the color of the tree in the foreground (muted though it is).

Objects nearby appear	Objects farther away appear
✦ In the foreground	✦ In the background
✦ Larger	✦ Smaller
✦ Brighter	✦ More muted
✦ More detailed	✦ Less detailed
✦ More textured	✦ Less textured

Even though the characters in the foreground are quite small (being seen from a distance), compare their size to the size of the train in the background. Everyone knows how huge a real-life train is compared to the size of a person. Drawing the train in the picture smaller than the characters in the foreground informs the reader that the train is very far away indeed. Through applying these basic principles, Schoenherr creates a magnificent sense of depth and a great expanse of space beyond what just a long-distance big-picture view alone might convey. Without applying these principles to create depth, an artist could create a big-picture view that appears relatively flat or one-dimensional.

Drawing the Reader In

Schoenherr uses another visual tool to engage the reader: implied or actual diagonals that draw the eye into the picture. Scanning the page, the eye naturally falls on the big red barn (the largest object with the brightest color) and then moves to the nearby cluster of buildings in the foreground. Having spotted the characters, father and child as they leave the house (in the lower left-hand corner) and the largest tree (also in the foreground), the reader's eye is then drawn diagonally back in a zigzag fashion along stone walls, wire fences, ridges of plowed fields, and tree lines as they all converge on a stream of light near the horizon. That stream of light is actually steam flowing from a distant train, which is apt to go unnoticed until the reader reaches the very last line of the text: "Somewhere behind us a train whistle blew, long and low, like a sad, sad song." Those words identify the train and call attention to the steam spilling out of the engine about the same time the series of diagonals draws the eye back to it. The timing is impeccable—and surely no accident.

Analyzing the Lead Sentences

After the students look at this first illustration and discuss all the information that Schoenherr conveys in the picture, I suggest reading the entire page aloud once through without stopping. Hold the book facing out as you read so students can keep their eyes focused on the picture while they listen to the words. This gives them the experience of taking in visual and verbal information at the same time and will help them understand how the words and pictures work together to deepen the meaning.

Ask students to share their experience of processing words and pictures together. Some students may tell you that they heard the train whistle blow or that they could feel the chill of the night. Whatever students do say, it should become clear that the words and pictures work together to make the picture come alive.

Following the reading of the first page of text, I find it helpful to reread the text, line by line, so that students can analyze the information Yolen provides as she sets the stage for her story. After I read each line, I pause to ask students to name the kind of information conveyed.

The discussion usually goes like this:

"It was late one winter night": *What did you find out?* (Time of day and season.)

"Long past my bedtime": *What did you find out?* (Time of day.)

"When Pa and I went owling": *What did you find out?* (Who the characters are and what they are doing.)

"There was no wind": *What did you find out?* (Weather and mood.)

"The trees stood still as giant statues": *What did you find out?* (Setting detail and mood.)

"And the moon was so bright the sky seemed to shine": *What did you find out?* (Time of day and setting detail and mood.)

"Somewhere behind us a train whistle blew like a sad, sad song": *What did you find out?* (Introduces sound and enhances mood; the sound of the train foreshadows the hooting of the owl, providing a subtle hook.)

The exercise of analyzing the first page of *Owl Moon* makes it clear how Schoenherr's lead picture does an excellent job setting the stage for the story. Yolen's lead sentences complement and enhance the picture by providing important details about the setting and the characters that could not be conveyed by the picture alone, while helping to establish the mood. The words make the pictures come to life and the pictures deepen the meaning of the words. Together, words and pictures create fuller power of expression than either language alone is able to convey. They also create a sense of "being there" as readers take in all the sensory, visual, and verbal information.

Notice how as readers encounter the words about the train (a hidden visual detail), they search the lead picture in an attempt to make sense of what is being heard and what is being seen. Once they spot the train, they can almost hear its whistle "long and low, like a sad, sad song." Yolen's use of sensory information, in this case sound, cleverly attunes readers' ears to the sounds of the night and prepares them to listen for the sound of the owl later in the story. The distant train whistle also fills the implied space and enhances the sense of depth established by the visual details on this page.

Changes in Perspective

As the story unfolds, Schoenherr uses another simple visual tool to draw the reader in, something I refer to as "changes in perspective." This concept is easy to understand if you begin by revisiting the first illustration. Notice the size of the characters on the first page of the story (Figure 8.3). They are relatively small. Over the next several pages (as the reader enters the story), Schoenherr depicts the characters larger and larger (Figures 8.4 and 8.5). He draws the reader into the story by making the characters appear closer and closer. By the fourth illustration, Schoenherr depicts the characters much bigger, bringing readers much closer to the characters just as the plot thickens. Readers may feel as though they are standing right there with the characters as they are drawn into the story.

Schoenherr continues to play with changes in perspective throughout the story. Sometimes he depicts the characters smaller (further away) and enveloped in the forest setting; sometimes he shows them

I could hear it
through the woolen cap
Pa had pulled down
over my ears.
A farm dog answered the train,
and then a second dog
joined in.
They sang out,
trains and dogs,
for a real long time.
And when their voices
faded away
it was as quiet as a dream.
We walked on toward the woods,
Pa and I.

Figure 8.4.   Father and child walking toward gate (and the reader).

so close that the expressions on their faces are easy to read. Sometimes Schoenherr depicts the characters from the point of view of someone on the ground; sometimes he depicts them as if seen from above, again hinting at the presence of a pair of watchful eyes overhead.

At the height of the drama, when father and child spot the owl, Schoenherr uses a dramatic change in perspective: a close-up of the owl, looming large overhead (Figure 8.6). Readers see the owl just as

Figure 8.5.   Fourth illustration: drawing the reader into the story.

the characters do, as if looking out of the characters' eyes. We find our-selves staring into the gleaming golden eyes of a very large owl; we feel the same flutter of excitement as the characters do when they spot the owl for the very first time. Notice how Schoenherr's use of the close-up serves to heighten the drama and build suspense. He also shifts from the third person (the reader watching the characters) to the first person (the reader looking out of the eyes of the characters) to fully engage readers in the story at the peak moment.

Figure 8.6.   Close-up perspective and shift to
"visual first person."

At the very end of the story, as Schoenherr prepares to conclude the
tale, he pulls back, using a small mid-range perspective that serves to
distance the reader from the characters (Figure 8.7). He also depicts the
father and child, their backs turned, heading home—to where the story
began. Notice the small house in the distance. If you look really closely,
you can see a tiny light in the window. Once spotted, the light draws the
reader's eyes toward the characters' final destination: home. Schoenherr
walks the reader out of the story "on silent wings under a shining Owl
Moon" (Yolen's words).

When you go owling
you don't need words
or warm
or anything but hope.
That's what Pa says.
The kind of hope
that flies
on silent wings
under a shining
Owl Moon.

Figure 8.7.   Final illustration.

Interlude: Changes in Perspective in Film

While book illustrators and videographers use changes in perspective all the time, this visual tool often goes unnoticed. Once you become aware of it, you begin to notice how illustrators and videographers intentionally manipulate what you see and how you see it (that is, from what angle and perspective) in order to subtly play with your emotions as they move you in and out of a story or a film. Film also uses sound, music, and movement to that end.

Next time you watch a movie, notice how the videographer artfully manipulates the viewer through changes in perspective. Consider the classic lead segment of a movie in which the videographer introduces the setting by showing the viewer panoramic shots of scenic vistas. These long-distance shots offer a wide-angle view and serve to establish the setting. You may notice the camera then zooming in on something small in the distance, often something moving, such as an automobile driving along a winding road, or one or more people engaged in an activity. To establish what is happening in the film and introduce the characters, the videographer needs to draw the viewers in closer, so they can see what is happening.

During moments of high drama, notice how the videographer often uses short-range shots to bring you up close and personal. Close-ups of the characters' faces make it easy to see their expression of emotion and are often used to heighten drama or build suspense. If the drama involves a large event such as a forest fire or a storm, however, the video-grapher may pull back to show the big picture and the magnitude of the problem or may move back and forth between extreme perspectives. As in *Owl Moon*, these changes in perspective become part of the very fabric of how the story is told.

Wild Horse Winter: Another Look at Visual Elements

Wild Horse Winter, written and illustrated by Tetsuya Honda (1992), is a book I often use to teach students about three simple visual tools that illus-trators use to make meaning as well as help to establish and heighten the mood in a story: color, texture, and changes in perspective. (See Figure 8.8.)

Changes in Perspective

In *Wild Horse Winter* Tetsuya Honda provides many artful examples of changes of perspective as he tells his story of wild horses that face many challenges as they make their annual winter journey to the sea. Like Schoenherr, at the height of the drama (when the horses are caught

Figure 8.8.   Cover of *Wild Horse Winter.*

in a terrible blizzard), Honda moves in closer, providing the reader with a close-up view of the panic-stricken expressions on the horses' faces as they struggle to keep their heads above the snow. Looking at that close-up perspective, you feel as if you are there with the horses in the storm (Figure 8.9).

Alternatively, when Honda wants to show the vastness of the horses' journey, he pulls way back, showing the horses traveling long distances across a vast salt marsh (Figure 8.10). This long-distance view is from above, much like the opening picture in *Owl Moon*. This time the scene is being viewed from the eyes of seagulls (or so it is implied), suggesting that the horses are getting closer to their destination: the sea.

Like Schoenherr, at the end of the story Honda leaves readers with a mid-range perspective, showing the wild horses galloping along the ocean shore (Figure 8.11). Both illustrators prepare for the story's ending by pulling back from a closer view, thus distancing the reader and helping to dissolve emotional ties with the characters. This sensitive change in perspective artfully draws readers out of the story at the end of each book.

Figure 8.9.   Close-up of horses in storm used to heighten the drama.

Figure 8.10.   Long distance view of horses used to show immensity of
their journey.

After their feast, the horses galloped along the beach. The colt raced behind them.

Figure 8.11.   Final illustration: use of mid-range perspective to pull
reader back from the drama.

Use of Color and Texture

In *Wild Horse Winter,* Honda employs two additional visual elements,
color and texture, to artfully craft his story. He uses these elements to
heighten the drama and build suspense as well as to establish a sense of
relief. While Honda's lead picture clearly establishes a "blue-sky mood,"
in succeeding pages the skies darken as night, and then the storm
approach. The colors of his illustrations deepen as daytime blue darkens
to deeper blues and then to the deep purples of twilight and the steely
dark blues of night. With the darkening of colors also comes the darkening of the story's mood. The sense of drama builds.

Honda also artfully utilizes texture to heighten the drama. With the
first signs of the storm, he adds texture in great sideways sweeps across
the page to introduce snow blown by strong winds, creating an almost palpable sense of motion. Notice the difference in mood between Figure 8.12
(the horses traveling before the storm arrives) and Figure 8.13 (the horses
traveling into the storm). Honda builds intensity through the addition of

Figure 8.12.   Horses traveling before the storm.

The wind was so strong that the colt could barely move. He followed in the footprints that his mother left in the deep snow.

Figure 8.13.   Horses traveling into the storm.

texture and the use of a closer perspective. He also adds dramatic tension through his skillful depiction of the horses' body language as they push into the storm, struggling to move forward on their journey.

Over the next several pages in the book, culminating in the scene shown in Figure 8.9 (also color plate P), Honda depicts increasing amounts of texture created by a thickening of the swirling snow, added to the increasingly dark colors of the night sky, which serves to further heighten the drama. The added texture also conveys a feeling of intensifying agitation and unrest. As Honda zooms in, he draws the reader in closer and closer to the drama of the horses being trapped in the snow.

When I lead a book walk with students, we discuss how Honda builds drama and suspense through the combined use of three visual tools:

✦   He darkens the colors of his illustrations to create a dark mood.

✦   He adds texture to create a feeling of agitation and unrest.

✦   He moves in closer so readers can see the distressed look on the horses' faces.

Honda also uses these same three visual elements—color, texture, and perspective—to establish a sense of relief. For instance, he moves from the dramatic sequence of pictures of the raging snowstorm (high texture), which peaks with Color Plate P to the calm after the storm (relatively little texture) as shown in Color Plate Q, clearly indicating a dramatic shift in mood from one of agitation and struggle to one of quiet and peace. Note the dramatic shift in mood that texture alone (or lack thereof) can create even when the colors remain cool and relatively dark.

On the next page (see Color Plate R), Honda abandons the dark, cool colors of night as he moves the reader into the early morning hours with the intense golden (warm) colors of a bright sunlit morning. With this drastic change in color, the shift in mood is clear, striking, and dramatic. It spells relief. (With my young students, I talk about that "sense of phew.")

As discussed earlier, throughout the story, Honda uses changes in perspective to heighten the drama as well as move the reader in and out of the story. As he prepares to end the story, he pulls the reader back away from the horses with a mid-range view and positions the horses to race right off the page and out of the story. Honda also paints a bright orange and golden sky that creates a warm, joyous feeling. His final picture conveys great warmth, joy, and excitement as the horses gallop along the shoreline "into the sunset" (Color Plate S). Anyone, speaking any language, understands that this is a happy ending.

Summary of Some Basics

Even for teachers with little or no art background, understanding a few simple concepts and introducing the vocabulary to talk about them, will make it possible to support students' growing visual literacy (reading of pictures). It will also enhance their meaning-making efforts as they create their own pictures. I find myself returning to three basic visual elements over and over again—and successfully teaching them to students as young as first grade.

Color

Warm colors (yellow, gold, oranges) create a warm feeling. Cool colors (such as blues and blue violets and blue greens) create a cool or cold feeling. *Wild Horse Winter* provides striking examples of the impact of color on mood.

Dark colors darken the mood of a picture or convey a somber or scary feeling. Bright colors convey a positive, happy feeling. This is also apparent in *Wild Horse Winter*.

Muted (pale or grayed-down, or both) colors create a quiet, peaceful feeling, which will vary in mood depending on whether warm or cool colors are used. The first illustration of *Owl Moon* shows the sense of peace and tranquility that muted colors can evoke as the cool blues and blue-grays invite the eye to rest on a largely textureless expanse. Likewise, the muted cool blue-green tones on the page after the storm in *Wild Horse Winter* convey a sense of tranquility (again with relatively little texture). In *Secret Dawn,* a book you see me use in a mini-lesson in the Artists/Writers Workshop Overview in the DVD, the warm, muted pastel pinks and lavenders also convey a sense of quiet and peacefulness but with a very different feeling compared to the one evoked by the cool colors used in *Owl Moon*.

Texture

Texture can be used to create a sense of movement, agitation, or unrest. Lack of texture conveys the opposite, a sense of peace and tranquility. An image without a lot of texture suggests relative calm and stillness.

Examples of this appear in *Wild Horse Winter* during and after the storm.

Perspective

A long-distance perspective helps convey a sense of setting by stepping back to view more of the place, the big picture. Using a mid-range view, the artist is able to show more of what is happening at that point in the story, helping readers understand the action or plot. A close-up view can serve to build drama and suspense. A close-up of a face (human or animal) lets readers see the expression on that face and become more attuned to the character's emotion. With the use of a close-up, the reader is literally drawn into the story. Pulling the reader away from the action and the characters at the end of the story serves to distance the reader, preparing the reader to leave the story as we saw in both *Owl Moon* and *Wild Horse Winter*.

A long-distance view can be used to convey the magnitude of a problem, especially one that affects a large area. Changes in perspective appear throughout *Wild Horse Winter* and *Owl Moon*.

The Pup's Rescue: One Student's Use of Visual Elements

Jared, a second grader who participated in Artists/Writers Workshop, created a research-based story about his favorite New Hampshire animal, the fox, during an integrated curriculum Picturing Writing project. Many of the visual elements and literary concepts that he and his classmates discussed during their many Literature Shares found their way to the pages of his carefully crafted tale, *The Pup's Rescue*.

Cover Picture

During Artists/Writers Workshop, Jared learned that the book title and the cover picture share the same job: to tell what the book is about and to whet the reader's interest.

In his cover picture (Figure 8.14), Jared introduces his family of foxes and provides some information about where the story takes place. He captures the reader's curiosity by giving the three foxes rather large eyes. The foxes appear startled, as if they have just heard a strange noise.

This picture, combined with the title, *The Pup's Rescue,* lets the reader know that something exciting is about to happen.

Jared also had an additional task when creating his cover picture: to integrate some facts he learned about his fox. Whether the initial information came from written or visual research, Jared conveys several

Figure 8.14.   Cover picture for *The Pup's Rescue* by Jared, grade 2.

important facts: foxes are nocturnal; foxes live in dens; a fox pup lives with its mother and father.

The dark night sky, the full moon, and the shadowy trees combined with the startled look on the foxes' faces all serve to establish an eerie mood on Jared's cover.

Lead Picture

In his three-page story, Jared displays the thoughtful use of changes in perspective and color. His lead picture (Color Plate U), designed to establish a sense of setting and introduce his character, uses a mid-range perspective. This enables Jared to provide important visual information about the setting (time of day, weather, season, and place) as well as to introduce the main character clearly enough so that readers can tell what the fox is doing. With his choice of a mid-range picture of his character, Jared is able to include facial details such as "eyebrows" that allow him to make the fox pup appear worried. This small visual detail serves as a hook, foreshadowing the danger to come.

Lead Sentences

Jared supports the visual details in his picture by providing important information within his text. Interestingly, if you asked Jared, he would tell you that he got his words from looking at his picture, yet his words go well beyond his picture in the telling of his story:

One windy summer night, a fox pup wandered away from his den in a tree trunk on the edge of a forest. The hungry pup was searching for food. As he sniffed the air, he heard a rock fall. He started to shiver. He felt scared.

Notice how Jared enhances the mood in his story through adding supporting sensory details that could not be conveyed by the picture alone. This provides a clear example of how engaging in art before writing serves to draw students into the story and experience its events as if they were there. Had Jared not been drawn into the story by his painting, I doubt he would have been able to access such rich sensory description.

Having discussed and analyzed several lead sentences during multiple Literature Shares, Jared remembers not only to set the stage for his story by including setting information but also to create a hook to ensure that the reader wants to turn the page. He writes, "As he sniffed the air, he heard a rock fall. He started to shiver. He felt scared." These words, which complement and support the worried look on the fox pup's face, foreshadow an unknown presence and the danger to come, capturing the reader's attention.

Problem Picture

On page two of his story, Jared creates a close-up to depict the problem in his story: a hungry coyote has spotted the young fox pup (see Color Plate V). Having learned from his study of *Owl Moon* and *Wild Horse Winter* that a close-up perspective can help to create suspense and drama, Jared searched the classroom library for a picture that would help him create a close-up. He found just what he wanted in Gail Gibbon's book *Wolves* (1994). While not about coyotes, the book gave Jared a rough idea of how to create a close-up of his coyote's head.

In choosing to create a close-up of the fierce coyote, Jared gives the reader the opportunity to look directly into the glaring eyes of the predator—as if the reader were the young fox pup himself. This enhances the reader's sense of how the young fox pup must feel. Like Schoenherr's image of the large owl as seen from the eyes of his main characters, Jared's perspective has shifted from third person (viewing the fox pup) on the first page to first person (viewing the coyote from the eyes of the fox pup) on his problem page. The reader is forced to stare directly into the fierce golden eyes of the coyote in much the same way the reader was positioned to stare into the intense yellow eyes of the owl in *Owl Moon*. Jared also chooses to darken his sky on his problem page, just as Honda and Schoenherr did in *Wild Horse Winter* and *Owl Moon*, respectively, to build suspense and heighten the drama. This serves to intensify the ominous mood. With this choice, coupled with his close-up of the coyote's face, Jared successfully creates suspense, the strong sense of impending danger. The full moon and suggestion of clouds in the darkening night sky serve to enhance the mood.

Writing to the Problem

Jared has also learned to craft his words carefully. Following a mini-lesson in which students analyze how authors create suspense and drama when writing to the problem, Jared thoughtfully selects his words:

> Suddenly, he came out to an open field where there was a coyote that was hungrily staring at the pup with his golden eyes. The starving coyote was ready to charge at the young pup.

With a clear sense of purpose, Jared chooses to use words like *suddenly, hungrily, staring, starving,* and *charge.* Like many of his classmates, he is proud not only of his pictures, but of his use of "silver dollar words" to create drama and suspense. He has learned to craft his language for a purpose.

Solution/Ending Picture

On page three of his story, Jared returns to a mid-range perspective as he depicts his solution (see Figure 8.15). Like Schoenherr, whose depiction of his characters at the end of *Owl Moon* serves to walk the reader out of the story (Figure 8.7), and Honda, whose final image has his horses headed off the page and out of the story (Figure 8.11), Jared also prepares his audience to leave his story. To accomplish this, he finds visual support in another illustration in Gail Gibbons's *Wolves* to help him carry out his idea. He depicts his fox pup and fox dad racing off the page and out of the story, with the coyote's tail all that remains of the fierce predator. In his decision to craft this image in this way, Jared prepares the reader to leave the story, the coyote literally leading the way. His choice of a mid-range perspective also serves to pull the reader away from the intensity of the up-close drama. We saw this same technique used in both *Owl Moon* and *Wild Horse Winter.*

Jared thoughtfully places the fox pup and its father on the other side of the same tree that appears on the first page (showing a change in location) and depicts the moon as having moved across the sky over time. Notice that the moon on both his problem and solution pages has a similar location—which, of course, conveys that not much time

Figure 8.15.   Jared's final image.

has elapsed between the imminent danger and the father's rescue of the pup. On his solution page, Jared also chooses to lighten the sky. This serves to create a lighter, less ominous (dark) mood. It signals the resolution of the problem and helps to create a sense of relief.

Writing to the Solution/Ending

Jared supports his final picture with the following text:

> Just then, the protective father leaped out from the den to rescue the pup. He showed his sharp teeth to the coyote. He growled fiercely, ready to charge at the coyote. The scared coyote fled to find something to eat in the field. The pup raced to the den with his father where he would be safe and protected.

Here Jared shows a sensitivity to sustaining the drama through his use of descriptive language (using words and phrases like *leaped, sharp teeth, growled fiercely, scared,* and *fled*) and also shows an interest in creating a sense of relief and resolution at the end of his story (using words like *safe* and *protected*).

Since Jared is only in second grade, his ability to create detail in his writing, to "paint pictures with his words" and to address the key elements of story in both pictures and words, may seem precocious. Clearly, Jared has benefited from the many literature-based mini-lessons his teacher presented on both the art of creating pictures that tell the story and the art of using words to paint pictures. With a big grin on his face, Jared explains his success: "We looked at books and they 'exspired' me to make a better picture within myself."

9 Mini-Lessons

Painting to Writing

It was fun painting my pictures because it took me into my story and I could imagine it.

—Chelsea, Grade 2

This chapter is designed to provide teachers with enough guidance to experiment with Artists/Writers Workshop in their classrooms. The lessons it presents are the introductory lessons from the Picturing Writing "Time of Day" unit, a teachers' manual designed to introduce basic crayon resist art skills to students, while enhancing their ability to write descriptive passages. The writing described in these lessons will support students in developing a sense of setting and mood in a piece of writing.

While these mini-lessons are not identical to those featured on the DVD, the introduction to watercolor on wet paper and crayon resist lesson on the DVD are very similar. The Artists/Writers Workshop Overview on the DVD follows a similar format while focusing on a different time of day.

Introduction to Watercolors

In Artists/Writers Workshop, we paint pictures with real artists'
paints and make books full of silver dollar words.

—Nicole, grade 2

✦ Theme: The job of the artist

✦ Literary Focus: Seeing the world

✦ Art Focus: How to use watercolors—exploring with paint

✦ Medium: Watercolor on dry paper and watercolor on wet paper

✦ Book: *I Am an Artist* by Pat Lowry Collins

✦ Art Materials

- 7" white cardstock
- #10 watercolor brushes
- Prang oval 16-color watercolors
- plastic containers for rinse water (two different sizes)
- half-sponges for wetting paper
- newspaper
- pencils

✦ Miscellaneous Materials

- Artists Frame
- TACKtab or Clear Mounting Squares to hang painting in Artists Frame

Note: While the size of the paper is not critical to the process, it does need to be coordinated with the size of the Artists Frame. The Artists Frame should create approximately a half-inch black border around the finished painting. See notes on constructing an Artists Frame in Appendix B.

Literature Share/Discussion

Read *I Am an Artist* by Pat Lowery Collins. After reading, ask the students, *What is an artist?* Collins writes "I am an artist whenever I look closely at the world around me." *Does this book tell us that an artist is someone who can produce fine artwork? An artist is someone who pays close attention to the world around them.*

Sample of what to say to the class:

According to Pat Lowery Collins, we are all artists. Part of what that means is that we are going to be looking closely at the world around us. What else do you think it might mean?

Pause after each question and let the class explore the point briefly before moving on. It's always more meaningful when students explore these issues and come to their own thoughtful conclusions. (In later sections, the comments suggested for the teacher are followed by the kinds of answers students might offer as they respond to each question. The intent here is to provide readers with an idea of how discussion *might* go.)

We are also going to begin exploring a variety of art materials and techniques so that as we see our world, we can create pictures to show what we see.

Modeling Session

Introducing Artists Materials

Today we are going to practice using watercolor paints. How many of you have used watercolors before? These are quality paints. [Show a new box.] One important job for artists is to learn how to take care of their paints so they last a long time and can be used again and again. Can anyone think of one really important thing I will need to remember when I am using watercolors?

I will need to wet my brush before I put it in the paint. I will also need to wash the paint off my brush before I choose a new color. Does anyone know why that is really important to remember? That's right, so my colors stay bright and don't become muddy. Whenever you paint, you will always have a container of water nearby so you can wet your brush and wash it between colors.

We will also be using special artist's brushes. It is important that we take good care of these brushes so we can use them again. Taking good care of our brushes means washing them off when we are done and placing them to dry standing upright in a container with the brush end facing up. [Demonstrate.] This way the brush will stay soft and will not get bent.

We are also going to use special cardstock paper that doesn't wrinkle when it gets wet. Because we are using artist's paper, I expect you to use it carefully and try not to waste it. As artists, we know it is important to use our materials carefully so they will last.

Even when we think we have made a mistake while we are painting, remember that we are always learning—that there really are no such things as mistakes. Whatever we do, we learn from. We call these "learning experiences." Sometimes when something surprising or unexpected happens that we like, we call it a "happy accident." During the year, we can share our learning experiences and our happy accidents with each other as we all learn together.

Today we are going to experiment with two kinds of paintings. One is painting on dry paper. The other is painting on wet paper. Let me show you how to paint on dry paper first.

Watercolor on Dry Paper Demonstration

What is the first thing I need to remember? I should always write my name on the back of my paper in pencil so my painting won't get lost.

Please write your name in pencil small in an upper corner of the paper—and write lightly, so if you do want to turn your paper over and use the back, you can erase your name.

What is the next thing I need to remember? I need to wet my brush. What color should I begin with? Watch how I am going to twirl my brush in the paint to make sure it has enough color on it. After these paints have been used a little more, they will be more moist and the paint will go onto the brush more easily.

Today is a day to just experiment. You don't have to make a picture of anything in particular. You can just choose a few favorite colors and fill your entire piece of white paper. What do I need to remember after I am done with one color? That's right, I need to rinse off my brush so I don't get the next color all muddy. Maybe I will use two or three different colors on this piece of paper. I might begin to notice which colors I think look good together. Artists are always making choices based on how they think it will look.

Can anyone guess what might happen if I keep putting layer upon layer of paint on this one piece of paper? My colors are going to turn all brown and muddy. If I want to keep my colors bright, here are two artists' tips: First, I need to remember to wash my brush between colors. And second, if I apply paint only where the paper is still white, my colors will not become muddy. So if I remember to wash my brush between colors and to paint only where the white spaces are, my colors will always be pure.

After I have filled all my white spaces, I am ready to place my painting on the newspaper to dry. It is important to know when it is time to stop painting.

Watercolor on Wet Paper Demonstration

Let me show you how to paint with watercolor on wet paper. First, I write my name small on a back corner of my paper. Then I dip this little half-sponge in clean water. Notice that I have two containers of water. One [identify it as being different from the other in size, shape, or color] is just for the sponge, and I will try to remember not to wash my brush in this container so I can keep the water clean. The other container of water is for washing my brush, and that water will become colored by the paint. Every once in a while, I will need to change the wash water.

At this point, it is a good idea to explain the procedure you would like your students to use to get clean water. Teachers of young children may want students to raise their hands when they are ready for clean water. Teachers of older students can explain how students can get clean water, whether it be at a classroom sink or a set of buckets—one empty and one full of clean water—at the side of the room.

Why do you think it is important to keep our sponge water clean?

Watch how I dip my sponge in the clean water and then squeeze it out so it is not too soggy. Then I am going to wet my whole paper. Notice how I am gently wetting the paper without rubbing the sponge over and over again on the surface. If I rub too much, I will begin to pull up little paper fibers that can be a problem later when I am painting. Notice how I am lightly drawing the wet sponge over my paper from left to right across the top, then again from left to right just below that wet area, and so on until my entire paper is wet.

After I have wet the paper, I will experiment applying paint to it. Watch this. What is happening to the paint when I paint on wet paper? Watch how the colors run together. I still need to remember to rinse off my brush every time I want to change colors. I also still need to fill in all my white spaces with paint and not put paint where I have already painted. Sometimes, my paint will spread or "bleed" onto areas where I have already painted. That is not a problem; it is one of the ways that watercolor on wet paper can create "happy accidents." Once I have filled in all my white spaces, that is a good time to stop. If I keep adding more and more paint to my paper, my colors will become muddy and I may even make a hole in my paper from wearing away the paper fibers. Learning when to stop is an important part of being an artist.

When I am done, I am going to carefully carry this paper over to the newspaper to dry. Notice how I need to carry it flat so that the paint does not run.

Work Session

Today you are going to make at least two paintings: one on dry paper and one on wet paper. If you have time, you may paint more paintings using whichever technique you like.

For now, you are just experimenting with paint. You don't have to be concerned about making pictures of things. In fact, I'd rather you just focus on selecting colors that you think look good together and practice your painting technique: washing your brush between colors, filling in the white spaces, and painting only where the white spaces are. Notice the difference between painting on dry paper and painting on wet paper. If you have time, you can make more than one painting using each technique, but try one of each technique first to make sure you have experimented with both of them. Remember, this is a time to explore and learn.

I am going to play some relaxing music while you paint.

Group Share

Ask a few students to each share one painting. Tack each painting to the Artists Frame (which you can create following the guidelines in Appendix B). An Artists Frame will honor the students' work as well as help bring focus to each painting. When it is time to share, ask each artist to sit in the Artists Chair, a designated seat of honor that has been placed at the back edge of the circle or group directly across from the Artists Frame. This enables the artist to look at the artwork while speaking.

Invite each artist to talk about the process of making the painting, whether it was painted on wet or dry paper and what colors the artist used. Use this opportunity to reinforce technical skills by asking questions such as, *Can you tell us how you were able to keep your colors so nice and bright?* or making statements such as, *Notice how Tom filled in all his white spaces and kept his colors nice and clean.* Ask students to comment on the differences between painting on dry paper and painting on wet paper. Invite each artist to call on two or three classmates for comments or questions. Group Share can be steered in a positive direction by inviting students to describe something specific they like about the painting (beginning their comment with "I like . . .") or asking a question (I wonder . . .").

As mentioned previously, it is important to keep a checklist of all those who have shared. One easy way to do this is to use a class list to record the date beside the name of each student who shares. This will assure students that they will get their turn. It also allows you to select artwork to share each day based on the following goals:

✦   Reinforce skills introduced.

✦   Share a "happy accident" or "learning experience."

✦   Honor individual students to boost their self-esteem.

✦   Make sure everyone gets a turn (over time).

For young students: Very young children may need more than one opportunity to explore with watercolors. On another day, during a second mini-lesson, you might model keeping the paint colors separate on the page (as opposed to all mixed together) once again, and then demonstrate creating a second painting where you mix all the colors together to get brown or black. You might ask:

Last time we were painting, did anyone notice what happens when we mix a lot of colors together or keep adding more and more paint? What should we do if we want to keep our colors bright? Wash the brush between colors and paint only where the white is.

Painting Twilight

As an artist, I think that the best artists paint the sky because it looks really beautiful so I was really happy that I was an artist who painted the sky.

—Fiona, Grade 3

- ✦ Theme: Twilight
- ✦ Literary Focus: Setting, time of day, and mood
- ✦ Art Focus: Colors of the twilight sky, watercolor on wet paper technique
- ✦ Medium: Watercolor on wet paper
- ✦ Book: *Grandfather Twilight* by Barbara Berger
- ✦ Art Materials
  - 7" white cardstock
  - #10 watercolor brushes
  - Prang oval 16-color watercolors
  - plastic containers for rinse water (two different sizes)
  - half-sponges for wetting paper
- ✦ Miscellaneous Materials
  - TACKtab or Clear Mounting Squares
  - Artists Frame
  - chart paper and marker
  - newspaper
  - pencils

Literature Share/Discussion

When we read I Am an Artist, *we talked about the job of the artist being to observe the world around us. How many of you looked at the sky today? Without looking, who can tell me what color the sky is today? Are there any clouds in the sky? What kind of clouds are they? What color are they? Did anyone notice what color the sky was when you woke up this morning?*

What happens to the sky at different times of day?

What are some words that tell about the different times of day?

Have your students name all the different times of day they know: *night, day, evening, afternoon, morning, noon, dawn, dusk, sunrise, sunset.* Write these words down on a piece of chart paper. If they miss some times of day, give them a few hints.

Has anyone ever heard the word twilight *before? I am going to read a book called* Grandfather Twilight *by Barbara Berger.*

After reading *Grandfather Twilight*, ask, *What time of day is twilight? When do we see a twilight sky? What happens to the sky at twilight? What is the mood of twilight? What colors does the sky turn?*
You may want to flip through the pages of the book as students try to recall the colors of the twilight sky.

Modeling Session

This lesson is modeled on the DVD: "Introduction to Watercolor on Wet Paper."
Demonstrate the use of watercolors on wet paper to paint twilight. Model wetting a piece of cardstock paper with a small sponge as you did the other day. Ask, *What colors should I use to paint twilight?* You may need to refer back to *Grandfather Twilight*.
The twilight colors are most often pink, purple (or violet), and turquoise. I like to show students how to paint the pink of twilight using the red violet in the paint box or what I call *magenta* as opposed to using the fire engine red (labeled red) in the paint box. Dip your brush in the water and twirl it in the selected paint color. Model how to stroke

the brush horizontally across the paper (and only partway across at times) so that the colors create the effect of clouds rather than solid stripes across the page. Observe how the paint runs when it is applied to wet paper. Model washing your brush in the rinse water before changing colors. Model allowing the paint to bleed or spread—again making an effort to apply the paint unevenly across the paper so that the painting does not resemble solid horizontal stripes. (You will notice some students painting stripes on the DVD.)

When you have filled in nearly all the white spaces, stop and ask your students if you are finished yet. Your students should tell you that you need to fill in *all* the white spaces. Model painting into the white spaces by spreading paint that is already on the paper if it is still wet. If the surface has dried, model using just a tiny dab of paint on the tip of your brush and *blending the color* into the existing paint. Do not leave any white spaces on your paper.

When you have filled in all the white spaces, turn your paper ninety degrees and hold it up. Ask your students whether this painting looks like the sky. (When turned ninety degrees, your painting should have a vertical look to it even if it doesn't contain painted stripes.) Ask, *Why doesn't this look like a sky?* Note how the vertical grain of your brushstrokes does not resemble the sky. Return the paper to the way it was painted (with horizontal strokes) and ask students if the painting now looks like the sky. Invite students to share their thoughts on why that is. (The horizontal strokes resemble clouds drifting across the sky.)

Work Session

Ask your students to paint pictures of the sky at twilight using watercolor on wet paper. Encourage individuality while staying within the science of what they have learned. Say something like

No two skies are ever alike and no two paintings should ever be alike. Think about what colors you would like to paint your twilight sky and how you will create that quiet peaceful feeling. I will play relaxing music to remind you of the feeling of twilight.

Group Share

Select two or three paintings to share, using the Artists Frame and the Artists Chair as before. Keep in mind the opportunity to reinforce skills that have just been taught as well as to celebrate diversity. Ask each artist, *Can you tell me what you were thinking as you created your painting?* Students may choose to discuss the colors they used, the way they applied the paint, whether their colors look soft or bright and why, what mood or feeling the painting creates. The artist may then call on two or three classmates for comments or questions. Comments should tell specifically what students like about the painting *and why* (not just "I like your picture"). Encourage questions about technique, such as "How did you get your sky to look like that?" or "What colors did you use for your sky?" You may also observe that some paintings have softer, lighter colors while others have brighter, bolder colors. Students can be invited to discuss how they accomplished each effect.

Watch for the opportunity to reinforce skills you've already taught.

I am noticing that Sarah did a nice job washing her brush in between colors. Notice how nice and clean her colors are.

I notice that Glenn remembered to fill in all his white spaces.

If there is time, you can invite students to brainstorm words to describe the particular sky in the Artists Frame. Write these describing words down on a piece of chart paper so the children can access them later. (At this point in the year, you may just be encouraging students to use silver dollar color words such as *magenta*, *turquoise*, and *violet*, instead of their five-cent counterparts *red*, *pink*, *blue*, or *purple*. It will be easier to access descriptive language once your students' paintings have more detail.)

If the painting looks like it has clouds in it, you can ask students what the clouds are doing. This question should elicit words like *drifting*, *floating*, and *sailing*.

You may also ask students to brainstorm words to tell about the mood, such as *peaceful*, *quiet*, and *serene*.

For older students: Older students can be introduced to the use of personification during the brainstorming session. Questions to invite use of personification might include: *If the sky were a person, what might it be doing at twilight?* This might elicit responses such as *going to sleep, pulling up its blanket of colors, drifting into dreams. . . .*

Note: Invite students to observe the sky at twilight for several nights. Ask them to take mental snapshots. Ask them to try to remember what colors are in the twilight skies they observe, how the colors change as time passes, and what happens to the clouds at twilight.

Writing to Twilight

Look at the picture for a long time and you kind of get into the picture and feel stuff, like if there is a breeze or something.

—Cooper, Grade 3

Note: You may prefer to move on without having the class try writing to this painting. Twilight paintings have very little detail to trigger the imagination and thus can be challenging to write about. The best use of this "Writing Strand" would either be simply brainstorming or possibly introducing haiku and writing a very simple three-line poem. Students in the second grade and up could pay attention to the 5-7-5 syllabic format.

+ Theme: Painting pictures with words
+ Literary Focus: Brainstorming or writing haiku poems, which could include personification
+ Art Focus: Painting pictures with words
+ Medium: Pencil and paper
+ Books
   • *Twilight Comes Twice* by Ralph Fletcher;
   • *The Sun's Day* by Beth Olshansky to introduce personification;

- *In a Spring Garden* by Richard Lewis (editor) to introduce haiku.
+ Miscellaneous Materials
  - Twilight paintings
  - Pencils
  - Writing paper
  - Easel stands
  - TACKtab or Clear Mounting Squares
  - Artists Frame
  - Chart paper and easel
  - Paper clips (large plastic preferred)

Literature Share/Discussion

Prepare to read the dusk section of *Twilight Comes Twice*—or the entire book—by introducing or reviewing the concept of personification. Then ask students to raise their hands every time they hear an example of personification. Discuss the impact of the language on the viewer. Ask students to close their eyes while you reread a sentence or two that uses personification. Ask students whether personification helps paint a picture in the reader's mind.

Alternative book: Read *The Sun's Day*. This is a crayon resist book I made to teach personification as well as other figures of speech. Discuss personification as described above. Ask students to stare at the picture as you read the text and notice if anything happens to the image.

If you are going to ask your students to write haiku, read a few examples from *In a Spring Garden* and discuss haiku as a poetic form.

Modeling Session

Practice brainstorming silver dollar words and phrases to describe the sky and the clouds. Since the twilight painting has few details, this is really just a warm-up. Encouraging personification will support accessing some descriptive language. If you choose to extend this lesson beyond the brainstorming, invite your students to help you select the best words and phrases, and then model creating a haiku as a group exercise. For grades 2 and up, model the 5-7-5 syllabic format, clapping or counting out the syllables.

Work Session

Following the Modeling Session for haiku, have students place their favorite twilight painting in their desktop easel stand and write a haiku about twilight. Play relaxing music as they write.

Group Share

Invite a few students to place their paintings in the Artists Frame and read their poems. Notice if their haikus make their paintings come to life.

Painting Sunset: Introducing Crayon Resist

I felt like I was becoming a real artist. . . .

—Dillon, grade 3

✦ Theme: Sunset
✦ Literary Focus: Setting, time of day, and mood
✦ Art Focus: Crayon resist art technique; interesting ground-line, foreground and background, difference in colors between sunset and twilight skies
✦ Media: Combined crayon resist and watercolor on wet paper

- ✦ Books
  - *The Legend of the Indian Paintbrush* by Tomie dePaola,
  - *The Sun's Day* by Beth Olshansky (show sunset and twilight pictures),
  - *Sun Song* by Jean Marzollo (wonderful picture of sunset over rolling hills),
  - *Grandfather Twilight* by Barbara Berger,
  - *The Oxcart Man* by Donald Hall (picture of twilight over an interesting ground-line)
- ✦ Art Materials
  - 7" white cardstock
  - #10 watercolor brushes
  - Prang oval 16-color watercolors
  - crayons
  - plastic containers for rinse water (two different sizes)
  - half-sponges for wetting paper
  - roll of toilet paper
- ✦ Miscellaneous Materials
  - TACKtab or Clear Mounting Squares
  - Artists Frame
  - chart paper and marker
  - newspaper
  - pencils

Literature Share/Discussion

To introduce sunset, read *The Legend of the Indian Paintbrush* by Tomie dePaola. (If not available, read *The Sun's Day* and develop a discussion along the lines of the one in the rest of this section but appropriate to that book.) The follow-up discussion to reading *The Legend of the Indian Paintbrush* may go something like this:

What was Little Gopher's gift to his people?

I believe that each of you carries a special gift inside just like Little Gopher's gift. Part of our work together will be to help you discover and develop your gift. Do you remember what helped Little Gopher fulfill his dream of painting the sunset?

Turn to the page that tells about his going to the hillside to watch the sunset.

I would like each of you to continue watching the sky at all different times of day and night. When you wake up, when you are riding in the car or on the school bus, when you are outside playing, try to remember to look at the sky. Watch the sky change colors when the sun is rising or setting. These can be magical times of day.

Some paint pigments originally came from berries and flowers just like the ones Little Gopher made. The brushes you are using come from animal hair just like the ones Little Gopher made. These special artists' materials will help you paint beautiful skies just like Little Gopher.

What did you notice about Tomie dePaola's paintings of the sunset? How do they differ from those we saw in Grandfather Twilight?

Open to a sunset page of the boy staring into the distance. Notice that the colors are a lot brighter, more fiery. Compare them to the softer, more pastel colors shown in *Grandfather Twilight*. For the purposes of this time-of-day study, define sunset as the time when you can actually see the sun setting and twilight as the time just after the sun has set when the bright colors of sunset begin to soften. During sunset, students will see at least part of the sun in the sky. During twilight, the sun has already set.

What else has Tomie dePaola included in his painting in addition to the sky? [Notice he has included the ground.]

Look at the way he has made his ground. Is it flat or hilly? Notice how he has made his hills to show that some are nearby and some are far off in the distance. Notice that the hills nearby are in the front or fore-ground and are larger. The hills in the distance are smaller to create a sense of depth. [Refer to one or more of these other books, if they're available: The Oxcart Man, Sun Song, or The Sun's Day.] How did these artists make their ground-line more interesting than just creating a straight line across the bottom of the page?

Note: Here I am introducing the concept of "interesting ground-line" in an effort to move students away from the proverbial straight line for ground that we see at the bottom of almost all children's representations of outdoor scenes. As you look at picture books, you will find many examples of "interesting ground-lines" to share with your students. (You will see me reinforcing this concept on the DVD several times.) You may also notice, and reinforce, that the sky actually touches the ground rather than being just at the very top of the page as often depicted by young children.

Modeling Session

We are going to experiment with a new technique today. It is called crayon resist. Has anyone tried crayon resist before? We are going to use crayon first and then paint over it with watercolor. Can anyone guess what might happen when I try to paint over crayon? Watch carefully.

Model using crayon resist to make a sunset picture. Begin using crayon to create an interesting ground-line. Let students know that you want to put in the ground-line so the viewer has information about where this particular sunset takes place.

What kind of place should I show? When you were younger, you probably made a straight green line for grass at the bottom of the page every time you made a picture of the outdoors. Now that you are older, what kind of ground-line would make a picture more interesting? Are we looking at the mountains when we see the sun setting? Or are we in the desert? Are we looking at gently sloping hills in the countryside or is the ground perfectly flat? What kind of place would allow me to make an interesting ground-line?

If students suggest you draw flat ground, ask how you might make that ground-line more interesting. You're looking for suggestions such as adding a butte or mesa to a desert landscape or a peninsula to the flat horizon of an ocean. After students respond, ask

What color should I use?

Model making an interesting ground-line, pressing down fairly hard with your crayon and then using your crayon to color or texture the ground to make it more interesting. On the DVD, you see me modeling coloring the mountains using the back of my crayon. This will create a texture that you can later paint over to fill in all the little white spaces that are created when coloring with crayon. If you are making mountains, you can model creating larger mountains in the front that are nearer and smaller mountains in the back that are farther away. This echoes what you noticed in some of the pictures discussed earlier.

If the sun is setting, will I see the entire sun or part of the sun? What color is the sun at sunset? What color crayon should I use? Where should I put the sun?

Since the setting sun is central to a picture of sunset, model finding a fairly central place to place the sun. I often model putting it in the nook created between two mountains as it just seems to beg to be placed there. Model coloring in the sun fully with crayon so that students will be able to do a quick watercolor wash right over the sun and the wax of the crayon will resist the paint.

Remind students that when doing crayon resist it is important to press down fairly hard with the crayons. Any white spaces within the crayon area should be filled in with paint later on to create a richer color and texture. It will be easier for young artists to completely color in their ground and the sun before painting the sky. Even if they do this, it is wise to ask them to paint over their ground to fill in all the grainy white spaces created by coloring with crayons.

Model finishing all the crayon detail before wetting the paper to paint.

Before modeling the painting, note that the colors of the sky may affect the colors on the ground. (Refer to pictures in *The Sun's Day,* in which the sunlight reflects on the mountains or the color of the sky reflects in the water. You can also see reflection of the sky in the water in Thomas Locker's *Water Dance.*) Model wetting the paper with the wet sponge going right over the crayon area. *If the sun is setting, what colors should I make the sky?* Model painting the sky first using horizontal strokes as students practiced with their twilight paintings.

Remember to paint the sky before *painting the ground. That way you will know what sky colors might tint the land or water below. After painting the sky to show sunset, paint over the ground area. Fill in all the white spaces with watercolors—even paint over the area where you already have crayon. This will allow the paint to seep into the little white grainy white spaces that remain when you color with crayons. The paint will enrich the colors and texture of the crayon areas.*

If students would like to add "tissue clouds" to their sunset skies, this must be done while the paint is still wet. For that reason, I model creating tissue clouds immediately after I have painted the sky—even before I paint the ground or water. Tissue clouds can be created by crumpling up one panel of toilet paper and pressing the bunched tissue into the freshly painted (still wet) sky. You will see me doing this in the Complete Crayon Resist Lesson on the DVD. I invite students to count to three with me as I press to help remind them that they must hold the tissue down long enough to absorb some of the wet paint. When I lift the toilet paper, a natural-looking cloud shape remains. With a quick twist of the crumpled tissue, I form a new cloud shape, which I then press into another wet area of the sky. Again, the students and I count to three. I repeat this activity as I create several tissue clouds spread across my sky.

When the sky has been painted (and tissue clouds added, if desired), it is time to focus on other parts of the picture. If the ground (mountains, hills, desert) has been entirely colored in, washing over it with sky colors will create the illusion of reflected light. If the ground has not been entirely colored already, students should select the appropriate color of paint to depict the kind of ground they have created. In a subsequent mini-lesson, I may introduce adding a body of water to the painting—which would provide me with the opportunity to talk about reflection of the sky on the water. You can also watch me model this on the DVD.

Key points in modeling crayon resist technique:

+ Press down fairly hard with crayon.
+ Finish all the crayon work before wetting the paper.
+ Wet the paper with a sponge before painting.
+ Paint the sky first.
+ Stroke the brush sideways as you paint the sky.
+ Wash the brush between colors to keep paints clean.
+ If you want to create tissue clouds, you must do so immediately after you have painted the sky, while the paint is still wet.
+ Fill in all the white spaces with paint, even where there is crayon.
+ Consider reflection or the effects of reflected light as you paint.

Work Session

Using the crayon resist technique just modeled, have your students paint one or two pictures showing sunset with some sort of "interesting ground-line." Play relaxing music while students paint.

Group Share

Select two or three paintings to place in the Artists Frame that show different interpretations of sunset or different kinds of interesting ground-lines. Follow the Group Share procedure described in the "Painting Twilight" mini-lesson.

Ask students to brainstorm "doing words" to tell what the sun is doing (such as *setting, sinking, slipping behind the horizon*) and "describing words" to describe the sun or sky. You may also encourage personification by asking, "If the sun were like a person, what might it be doing at this time of day?" Students may respond by saying, "going to sleep," "getting ready for bed," "drifting into dreams," whispering good night" and the like. Invite words that tell about the mood as well. Write these words on chart paper.

For older students: Older students can brainstorm describing words and phrases including similes, metaphors, or personification. Examples of these techniques:

- ✦ The sun slipped quietly behind the mountain like a fading memory.
- ✦ The sun melted into the fiery sky.
- ✦ The sun whispered good night as it pulled up its colorful quilt.

Writing to Sunset

The beautiful pictures gave me all kinds of ideas of what to write and that's how I got the idea [for my writing]. I think it is easier if you make your picture first instead of you just thinking. The pictures show you how to do it, like what to write and what not to write.

—Matthew, Grade 2

- ✦ Theme: Painting pictures with words
- ✦ Literary Focus: Writing descriptive passages and using similes, personification, and metaphor
- ✦ Art Focus: Painting pictures with words
- ✦ Medium: Pencil and paper

+ Books
  • *The Sun's Day* by Beth Olshansky or
  • *Twilight Comes Twice* by Ralph Fletcher
+ Miscellaneous Materials
  • Sunset painting
  • Pencils
  • Brainstorming sheet
  • Easel stands
  • TACKtab or Clear Mounting Squares
  • Artists Frame
  • Chart paper and easel
  • Paper clips (large plastic preferred)
+ Other Resources
  • *Quick as a Cricket* by Audrey Wood (similes)
  • *Mother Earth* by Nancy Luenn (personification)

Literature Share/Discussion

Read a story or a passage that includes rich, descriptive language. Discuss the literary devices used and the impact of the language on the viewer. I like to ask students to raise their hands whenever they hear an example of personification. Both *The Sun's Day* and *Twilight Comes Twice* will allow you to focus the discussion on personification. If you use *The Sun's Day,* have students stare at the picture as you read the text, and ask them to notice if anything happens to the image.

Modeling Session

I have divided this Modeling Session into two sections: first grade and then second grade and up, to allow you to better adapt this session to emergent writers. In either case, insert the class painting of sunset (your modeling painting) in the Artists Frame and tack up a piece of chart paper near it.

First Grade

When working with young students, write "sun" and "sky" on a piece of chart paper (or "sun," "sky," and "clouds"). Brainstorm silver dollar words and phrases for each noun. Encourage students to practice personification by asking, "at sunset, if the sun were like a person what might it be doing?" If you want to ask more concrete questions, you can say, "If the sun had eyes, what might it be watching? If the sun had ears, what might it be listening to? If the sun had a mouth, what might it be saying (and how would it be saying it)?"

For sky, ask, "What is the sky doing? What does the sky look like?" For clouds, ask, "What are the clouds doing?" "What do the clouds look like?"

Sample First-Grade Brainstorming List

Sun
+ Going to sleep
+ Getting ready for bed
+ Yawning
+ Sinking
+ Whispering good night
+ Setting

Sky
+ Blanketing the land
+ Looks like a colorful quilt
+ Looks like colorful blanket

+ Is painting a picture
+ Smiling
+ Changing color

Clouds
+ Floating
+ Drifting
+ Dancing
+ Wispy
+ Puffy
+ Fluffy

Ask students to select their favorite words or phrases and model how to write a simple sentence:

The sun is getting ready to sleep.

The sky makes a colorful blanket.

The clouds are drifting.

Write these sentences on an erasable board or on chart paper you can remove. First graders tend to copy whatever the modeled sentences are, so it is wise to remove them once you have modeled. The brainstormed words and phrases—which are their words—can remain in view. Some first-grade teachers have copied the brainstormed words onto a piece of 8.5"×11" paper and made copies of the words so that students have a word bank at their desks.

Ask students to write a sentence about each "thing" (noun) the class focused on during the brainstorming process. Emergent writers can be given sentence strips that look like this:

The sun_____.
The sky_____.
The clouds_____.

Some teachers like to add a line stating the time of day or a line which provides an opportunity for students to write what they are doing at that time of day.

It is_____.
or
I am_____.

Second Grade and Up

Model the brainstorming process using the graphic organizer described in Chapter Five. Appendix B includes a blank copy of the brainstorming sheet I use. Ask students to help you identify the four "most important things" in the class picture (nouns) and then brainstorm "doing words" (verbs) and "describing words" (adjectives). Also invite them to brainstorm "how words" (adverbs) as well as personification, similes, and metaphors, depending on their grade level.

Invite students to gaze at the painting while you read down one column at a time. Ask students to listen carefully and select the words or phrases that do the best job telling about the picture. Model circling these words and phrases. Discuss trying to create a unified mood.

Sample Brainstorming List, Grade 2 and Up

Sun
+ Going to sleep
+ Getting ready for bed
+ Yawning
+ Painting the sky
+ Whispering good night
+ Singing a lullaby
+ Slipping behind the mountains
+ Sinking behind the mountains
+ Slipping slowly
+ Setting

Sky
+ Blanketing the land
+ Looks like a colorful quilt
+ Looks like a painting
+ Is as colorful as a canvas

+ Blushing with color
+ Changing color

Clouds
+ Floating (slowly)
+ Drifting (silently)
+ Dancing
+ Wispy
+ Puffy
+ Fluffy

Mountains
+ Getting sleepy
+ Going to sleep
+ Whispering good night
+ Watching the sun set
+ Listening to the crickets
+ Sleepy

Ask students to dictate some descriptive sentences using some of their best words and phrases. Students do not have to use the circled words, but the process of circling words models selection, which is a very important skill in teaching the thoughtful crafting of language. Example of a first-draft dictated piece:

The golden sun is slipping behind the mountains. It is painting the sky. The fluffy clouds are drifting over the sleepy mountains. The mountains are watching over the valley below. The sun whispers "good night."

You can model revising this passage in the following ways:

+ Remove the helping verbs to make the verbs more active.
+ Remove extraneous uses of "the" or "and then."

✦ Find places to put adverbs or "how words" to enhance the mood.

✦ Create compound sentences.

Example:

The golden sun slips slowly behind the mountains as it paints the sky. Fluffy clouds drift lazily over the sleepy mountains. The mountains watch over the valley below. The sun whispers "good night."

Ask students to stare at the painting while you read the words. Ask them to see "if anything happens to the picture" as you read the words. Depending on the words in the passage, some students may see the clouds or the sun move. (If you want this to happen, try to tailor your descriptions to include active verbs, those that describe movement.)

Even if students don't see movement, they should be able at least to convey some sort of change in feeling about the image. Some students will tell you that the picture seems to "come to life" or you feel like "you are there, in the picture."

Note: This lesson can be extended by modeling how to turn a descriptive passage into a poem. Model removing (crossing out) all the small extraneous words and making slashes where you naturally pause when you read the sentences. Reformat the passage into a poem by copying the piece over and beginning a new line after each slash mark.

The reformatted poem will look like this:

Golden sun slips slowly
behind the mountains,
painting the sky.
Fluffy clouds drift lazily
over sleepy mountains.
Mountains watch over the valley.
Setting sun whispers "good night."

Work Session

Following the Modeling Session, have students place their favorite sunset painting in their easel stands, use the brainstorming sheet to brainstorm descriptive language, circle their best words and phrases, and then write to sunset. Play relaxing music.

Group Share

Invite a few students to share what they have written (accompanied by their picture, of course, placed in the Artists Frame). Remind classmates to stare at the painting while the words are being read to see "if anything happens to the picture." Invite positive comments and questions.

Note: Revision can also be addressed using the color-coding system described in Chapter Six.

10 Conclusion

The Power of Pictures

I just went berserk with joy.
I can't believe it ended up the way I never thought it would.
It's one of the best things that ever happened to me and I hope that it happens again.

—Andrew, Grade 3

I was visiting a school in a small New Hampshire town not too long ago, to offer coaching in several classrooms when Fern, a first-grade teacher, caught me in the hallway to tell me I shouldn't bother coming into her room. "I have the most active class I have had in thirty years," she told me. "They can't sit still. They don't listen. And they can't follow directions. I am afraid if you come in to paint today, it will be a total disaster." I had scheduled an hour for her, and I was not eager to give it up. "Just let me give it a try," I coaxed.

When I arrived, Fern had newspaper and paint boxes spread out on the tables, and her first graders were visibly excited. When I gathered them on the carpet to read a favorite picture book, they listened intently save for the occasional first-grade interruption to tell me about their new kitty or their new baby brother, but isn't that what first graders are all about? Except for one extremely talkative child who offered nonstop commentary, all the children stood quietly around my table as I modeled how to create a crayon resist painting.

When it came time to paint, I put on relaxing music as I always do. Fern's students became completely captivated by the crayon resist process. They were focused and attentive. I looked at Fern and the handful of teachers who had come to observe. They all knew what Fern's class was usually like. Now they saw her students fully engaged and following directions. Fern shrugged, a bit perplexed by this change in behavior. She leaned over to whisper, "Wait until you see them during writing time."

I didn't actually get to see them during writing time because I was not in school that day, but when I returned to the school two months later, Fern caught me in the hallway and ushered me into her classroom with a sweep of her arm. "Come here," she called out. "I have something to show you!" She directed me to a corner of her room where I spotted a plastic bin of her students' published books. "You have got to see these," she said, absolutely delighted. She flipped quickly through the books in the bin until she came to the one she was looking for. She grabbed the book and threw it on the table. "This," she announced, "is my lowest student. Look at this book."

She couldn't wait for me to pick up the book. She grabbed it and opened to the first page. "Look at this language." She flipped to the second page. "And this language. . . . Can you believe this personification? And look, here is a simile. . . . " Fern was obviously delighted. She grabbed a second child's book from the bin. "This," she announced, "is my second-lowest student. Look at what she wrote. . . . In my thirty years of teaching, I have never seen first graders write like this. And these are my lowest students." Kate, the teacher next door, had wandered into Fern's classroom. "I noticed the same thing in my classroom," she said, "I couldn't believe what my lowest kids were writing."

I was pleased by their observations, of course, but couldn't contain myself. "These books are wonderful. I am so glad to see that the process worked for you and your students. But we really need to stop referring to these kids as 'our lowest kids.' Just look at how capable these students are. Look at the writing they have produced!"

Conversations like this one are not unique, nor uncommon. I hear stories like this frequently from teachers while waiting in line for the copy machine, via e-mail, while passing in the hallways in schools or at teacher conferences—stories about the surprising work their "lowest students" have produced while using Picturing Writing or Image-Making. I think back to Thomas West's revelations about the hidden genius that is forced to lie dormant within some of our visual learners, those who are rarely given the opportunity to use their strengths in the classroom.

Over the last two decades, I have heard dozens, possibly hundreds, of stories from teachers who have discovered the power of pictures to capture students' imaginations, harness their energy, and provide them with a dynamic language for learning.

Just recently, while I was in the throes of final revisions of this book, I received a large envelope in the mail from a teacher in New Jersey whom I had never met. The envelope contained the following story and a color copy of the intriguing collage. With permission, I share this story with you as a final example of the power of pictures to transform the lives and learning of some of our most challenged and challenging students.

In January of his third-grade year, an English language learner in our school who was receiving multiple forms of academic support was being recommended for retention. Nothing about his performance in any content area gave any of his teachers even a glimmer of hope that he was absorbing anything he was being taught.

Silvio's class was participating in Image-Making in my enrichment class and, like his fellow students, he loved creating his portfolio of textured papers. Following the mini-lesson on image-finding, I was very busy moving about the room checking on individual students and, as always happens, before I knew it, it was time to clean up for lunch. Most students began cleaning up right away, but Silvio was still hard at work. Because *nothing* had ever come between him and lunch, I decided to allow him the extra few minutes he needed to finish his collage.

For the first time that day, I made my way to where Silvio was working, and what I saw literally took my breath away. With no assistance or guidance other than the same mini-lesson all the other students had received, Silvio produced an amazing collage image that displayed a sophistication of line, color, form, and balance not often seen in the work of an eight-year-old. His shapes were reminiscent of Matisse, but I would stake my life on the fact that he's never laid eyes on any of the works of the great artists. His use of positive and negative space, his placement of shapes, and his understanding of when to stop are elements that most who aspire to make art spend years trying to achieve (Color Plate T).

I rushed to the principal with Silvio's collage image in hand. She, too, was astonished by the image. I contrasted his work with several more typical third-grade collages and made my case that only an individual with the potential for high achievement could produce such a work. Whatever it was that was holding Silvio back from success in the more traditionally measured aspects of IQ, this image unequivocally demonstrated that he had potential. Silvio produced four more equally beautiful abstract images before he began his writing. At the end of his first writing session, as Silvio brought his folder up to be filed, he commented that he had finished his first page. Curious, after he had left, I pulled out his writing and, once again was rendered speechless. He'd filled half a page with beautiful, descriptive prose, telling the story of an orphaned fish who found himself in danger of being swallowed up by a fiery, haunted ocean. Not only did he use words like *terrified, exquisite, eerie, horrified, and scorched,* but he used them correctly! Once again, I tore down to the principal's office eager to share this amazing piece of writing.

I could not help but wonder whether Silvio's innate ability would ever have been recognized if not for the Image-Making process? Luckily we'll never have to find out. It was no surprise that his performance in other areas of the curriculum began to improve as well, not long after his collage book was published. Needless to say, the topic of retention was abandoned, with Silvio's Image-Making book a key piece of evidence in that decision. This student, who was basically condemned to an academic career driven by remediation, recently announced his plans to become a writer. Or a "math man." I have no doubt he can do both!

Don't be surprised if you, too, uncover hidden talents in some of your most challenging students, as you explore with them the power of pictures and create new pathways to literacy through art.

I invite you to join me in this quiet revolution.

Appendix A
Program Effectiveness

Research Results

Over the last two decades, I have been fortunate to have had three opportunities to look at the impact of art-based literacy and Artists/ Writers Workshop on a large scale. The research and standardized test score data was based on the implementation of two very specific art-based literacy models: Image-Making Within The Writing Process, the collage-based approach to literacy learning that I developed in 1990, and Picturing Writing: Fostering Literacy Through Art, developed in 1996, which uses crayon resist as a point of entry into the writing process. While the art processes serve as easy visual identifiers for each model, I need to empha-size that in no way do these research results suggest that a teacher who uses collage in the classroom or crayon resist as an art technique outside of the context of the comprehensive Artists/Writers Workshop approach I describe in this book will automatically duplicate these results. I hope it has become clear from reading this book and watching the DVD that the art process is the vehicle for introducing visual and kinesthetic thinking into the writing process, and that the entire Artists/Writers Workshop format offers a carefully designed progression of daily art-and-literature-based teaching practices that give students access to visual and kinesthetic thinking within the writing workshop model. I also do not claim that any art integration model will produce the kinds of results reported here.

Additional data as well as updates on current studies are available at www.picturingwriting.org/effectiveness.html.

The First Study: Image-Making Within the Writing Process

A quasi-experimental research study involving 377 first- and second-grade New Hampshire students in three schools from three different school districts was designed and conducted by Dr. Susan Frankel between 1991 and 1993. The study was designed to look at the impact of Image-Making Within The Writing Process on students' writing and use of art as a vehicle for communicating their ideas.

Pre- and post-test art and writing samples from first- and second-grade students in demographically matched treatment and comparison groups were scored by a team of independent raters. All students' writing was typed in a uniform fashion and scored apart from the artwork so as to ensure a blind study. Two scoring instruments were developed by a team of experts: one to look at students' use of visual elements to communicate their ideas and one to look at students' writing, specifically in the areas of story development and use of descriptive language.

The study documented significant gains in students' overall writing skills when participating in Image-Making Within the Writing Process over a three-month period as compared to the gains in writing made by students in demographically matched comparison groups over the same time period (see Figures A.1 and A.2). Specifically, the study documented significant gains in students' story development and use of descriptive language in the treatment group, as compared to smaller, or no gains made by students in the comparison group over the course of three months.

Significant gains in students' use of art as a vehicle for communicating their ideas were also documented, as shown in Figure A.3. As noted, only minimal gains in students' use of art were documented within the comparison group.

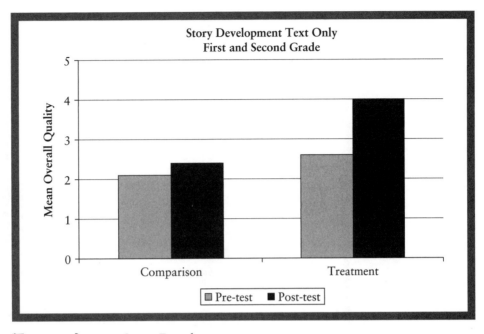

Figure A.1.   Story Development
1 = None; 2 = Minimal, traces; 3 = Abbreviated; 4 = Displays trait but not fully developed;
5 = Fully developed.

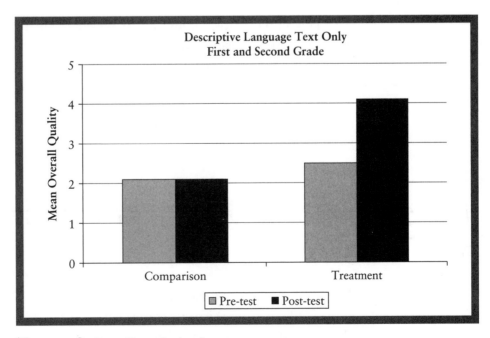

Figure A.2.   Descriptive Language
1 = None; 2 = Minimal, traces; 3 = Abbreviated; 4 = Displays trait but not fully developed;
5 = Fully developed.

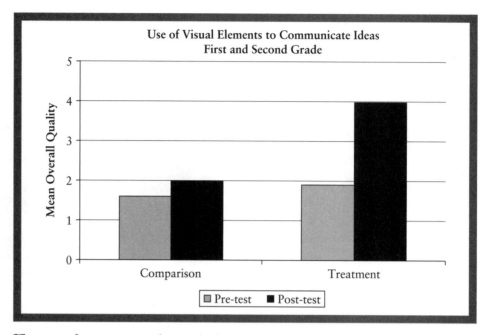

Figure A.3.   Use of Visual Elements to Communicate Ideas
1 = None; 2 = Minimal, traces; 3 = Abbreviated; 4 = Displays trait but not fully developed;
5 = Fully developed.

This initial study, submitted to the Program Effectiveness Panel of the National Diffusion Network, resulted in the validation of Image-Making Within The Writing Process as an "innovative and effective literacy program" in 1993, by the U.S. Department of Education. Subsequent federal funding through the National Diffusion Network supported national dissemination of Image-Making Within The Writing Process between 1993 and 1996.

The Second Study: Picturing Writing and Image-Making

A second quantitative research study involving 555 first- and second-grade students from thirteen schools across three states (New Hampshire, Hawaii, and Texas) was designed by Dr. Susan Frankel of RMC Research, Inc., to determine the impact of combining the two art-based literacy models (Picturing Writing and Image-Making) on student writing and the use of art as a vehicle for communicating ideas over the course of an entire school year.

School sites were carefully selected across the three states to ensure that participating students represented a range of geographic regions as well as socioeconomic levels.

Teachers in the treatment group agreed to implement Picturing Writing three times a week for sixty to ninety minutes per session from September through the end of January and Image-Making from February through the end of May. These teachers also agreed to follow a progression of detailed art-and-literature-based mini-lessons outlined in three Picturing Writing manuals and one Image-Making manual so as to ensure consistency of implementation. Teachers in the comparison group (from demographically matched classrooms) agreed to continue implementing whatever approach to writing they were currently using. Many, though not all, of the comparison classrooms were using a writing process approach to teach writing. Students in the comparison group were demographically matched to those in the treatment group based on each participating school's percentage of students on Free and Reduced Lunch Programs, geographic region, and population density.

Art and writing samples were collected in September, at the end of January, and at the end of May. For the writing study, all writing samples were separated from the accompanying artwork and typed in uniform fashion to ensure that a blind study was being conducted. Evaluating students' use of pictures to communicate their ideas was, of course, not a blind study.

To evaluate the use of the two languages (the language of pictures and the language of words), separate scoring instruments were required. The scoring instruments used in the preliminary quantitative study (1991–1993), which had passed the scrutiny of the National Diffusion Network's Program Effectiveness Panel in 1993, were used again. Art and writing samples were scored by a team of trained independent raters.

Research Findings

For the Text Only Study, shown in Figure A.4, both the treatment and comparison group demonstrated the same minimal overall writing ability (1.34) in September. By January, following five months of

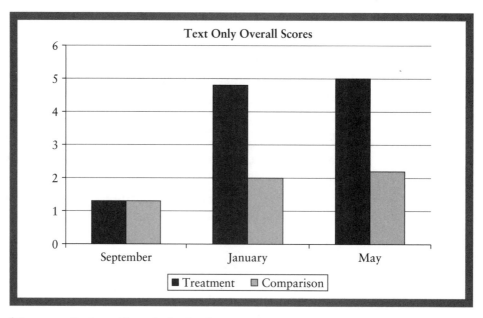

Figure A.4.   Text Only Study
1 = None; 2 = Minimal, traces; 3 = Abbreviated; 4 = Displays trait but not fully developed;
5 = Fully developed; 6 = Extraordinary.

Picturing Writing, the average score for the overall quality of student writing for the treatment group climbed to 4.80 (almost fully developed) while the average score for overall quality of writing for the comparison group increased to 2.03 (still minimal). By the end of May, following three months of the Image-Making process, the average score for the overall quality of student writing in the treatment group continued to increase to 5.04 (fully developed). The average score for the overall quality of student writing in the comparison group increased to 2.22 (slightly above minimal).

For the Visual Elements Study, which looked at how students used visual elements to communicate their ideas, the comparison group began the year in September with slightly more skill in using pictures as a language (1.97 for the comparison group as compared to 1.90 for the treatment group, see Figure A.5.) Both groups demonstrated less than minimal abilities. By the end of January, following five months of Picturing Writing, the treatment group's overall use and quality of visual information jumped to 4.07 (displays trait but not fully developed) while the scores of the comparison group remained minimal at 1.92.

By the end of May, following Image-Making, students' skills in the treatment group increased to 4.67 (almost fully developed) while the skills of students in the comparison group remained static at 1.92 (minimal).

In September, at-risk students in the treatment group began the year with marginally lower scores in overall quality of student writing (1.27) than their regular education classmates (1.40), as shown in Figure A.6. (At-risk students are defined as those identified as requiring Special Education or Title I services in the area of language arts.)

By January, the writing scores of at-risk students in the treatment group more than doubled those of the at-risk students in the comparison group (4.70 to 1.93), shown in Figure A.7, yet still marginally lagged behind those students in the treatment group who are not considered to be at risk (4.85).

By the end of May, as shown in Figure A.8, at-risk students in the treatment group achieved writing scores essentially equal to those students in the treatment group who were not identified as being at risk (5.00 to 5.04) and excelled far beyond the writing skills achieved by all students in the comparison group (2.22).

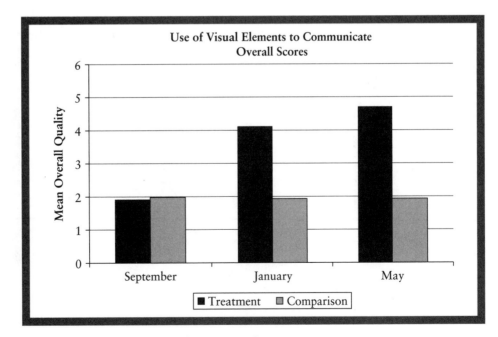

Figure A.5.   Visual Element Study
1 = None; 2 = Minimal, traces; 3 = Abbreviated; 4 = Displays trait but not fully developed; 5 = Fully developed; 6 = Extraordinary.

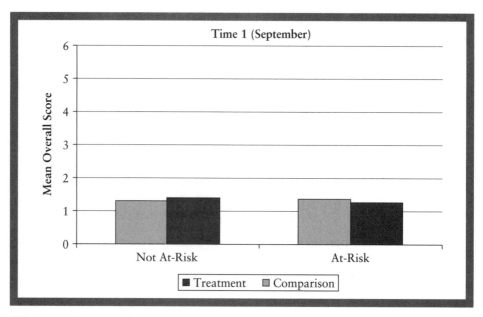

Figure A.6.   September Text Only Study
1 = None; 2 = Minimal, traces; 3 = Abbreviated; 4 = Displays trait but not fully developed;
5 = Fully developed; 6 = Extraordinary.

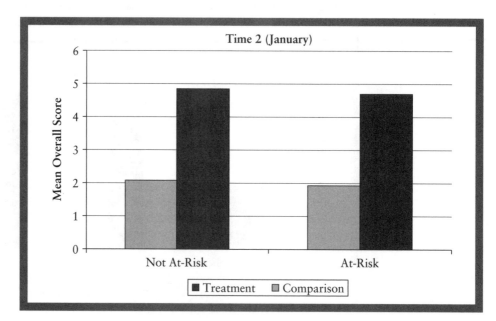

Figure A.7.   January Text Only Study
1 = None; 2 = Minimal, traces; 3 = Abbreviated; 4 = Displays trait but not fully developed;
5 = Fully developed; 6 = Extraordinary.

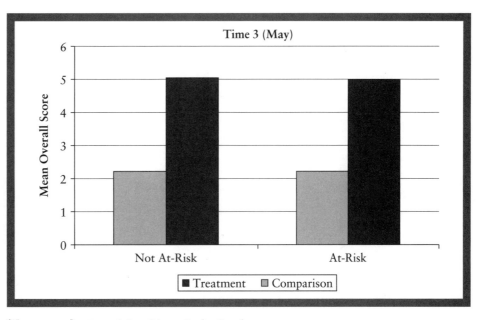

Figure A.8.   May Text Only Study
1 = None; 2 = Minimal, traces; 3 = Abbreviated; 4 = Displays trait but not fully developed;
5 = Fully developed; 6 = Extraordinary.

In the Visual Elements Study, at-risk students in the treatment group began the year with similar levels of skills to students who were not identified as being at risk in the treatment group (1.91), as shown in Figure A.9. Comparison group students (both at risk and not at risk) displayed slightly greater skills than students in the treatment group in their use of pictures as a language (1.95 and 1.97 respectively).

By January (Figure A.10), at-risk students in the treatment group displayed a strong foundation of skill in the use and quality of visual information as compared to at-risk and not-at-risk students in the comparison group (3.89 for at-risk treatment group as compared to 1.87 for at-risk students in the comparison group and 1.94 for those not at risk in the comparison group). January at-risk treatment students (3.89) still lagged marginally behind treatment students who are not at risk (4.22).

By the end of May, however, as shown in Figure A.11, at-risk students in the treatment group achieved scores marginally higher than students in the treatment group who were not identified as being at risk (4.68 to 4.66).

At-risk students in the treatment group also excelled far beyond students in the comparison group who were not identified as being at risk

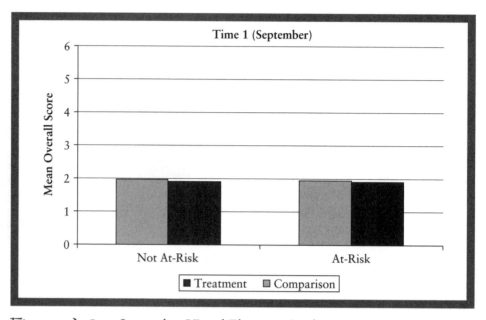

Figure A.9.   September Visual Elements Study
1 = None; 2 = Minimal, traces; 3 = Abbreviated; 4 = Displays trait but not fully developed;
5 = Fully developed; 6 = Extraordinary.

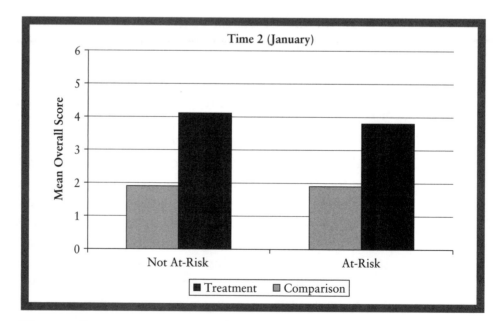

Figure A.10.   January Visual Elements Study
1 = None; 2 = Minimal, traces; 3 = Abbreviated; 4 = Displays trait but not fully developed;
5 = Fully developed; 6 = Extraordinary.

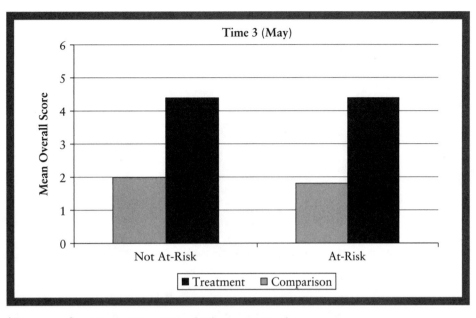

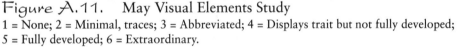

Figure A.11.   May Visual Elements Study
1 = None; 2 = Minimal, traces; 3 = Abbreviated; 4 = Displays trait but not fully developed;
5 = Fully developed; 6 = Extraordinary.

(4.68 to 1.99). At-risk students in the comparison group scored 1.74 as compared to at-risk students in the treatment group, who scored 4.68.

Because the 1997–1998 study built on the research model used in the 1991–1993 study, it was possible to compare the gains made by students who participated in Image-Making for three months (during the 1991–1993 study) to the gains made by students who participated in Image-Making following five months of Picturing Writing (during the 1997–1998 study), as shown in Figure A.12. Significant gains were documented for those students participating in a full nine-month art-and-literature-based approach to writing instruction as compared to those who participated for only three months (5.03 compared to 4.09). In this case, we can conclude that more is better.

Reading and Writing Standardized Test Scores

Based on the research findings described in the preceding sections, Main Street School in Exeter, New Hampshire, received a three-year Comprehensive School Reform Demonstration (CRSD) grant (1999–2002)

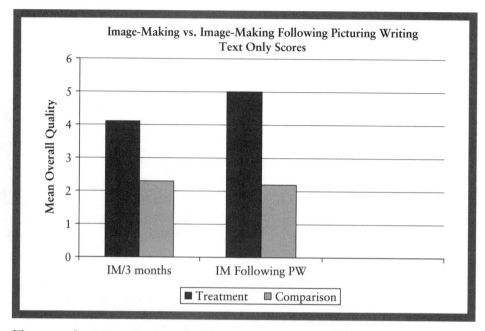

Figure A.12.   Art-Based Literacy: Three months versus nine months
1 = None; 2 = Minimal, traces; 3 = Abbreviated; 4 = Displays trait but not fully developed;
5 = Fully developed; 6 = Extraordinary.

to adopt Picturing Writing and Image-Making school-wide and integrate them into the language arts and science curriculum. The entire staff of eighty people participated in school-wide teacher training and implementation over the course of Year 1 (1999–2000); grade level teams then developed and implemented integrated curriculum science, language arts, and art units during Year 2; and during Year 3, classroom teachers refined their integrated curriculum units through continued implementation. Teachers facilitated Artists/Writers Workshop two or three times a week for between sixty and seventy-five minutes per session. No other writing programs and no new reading programs were adopted from 1999 to 2007.

This school-wide adoption created the first opportunity to gather standardized test data for an entire grade level (nine classes) over time. The tables in this section represent only a sampling of a larger pool of standardized test data from the Exeter School District (O'Connor, 2007), which is available at www.picturingwriting.org/effectiveness.html. Much of the data included in this section focuses on the standardized test scores of students identified for Title I and Special Education services.

✦ On the California Achievement Tests given to all second-grade students at Main Street School, the disaggregated data for Title I second graders shows overall increases in percentage of students scoring in the high and middle ranges and decreases in the percentage of students scoring below the national average over time. (See Table A.1.) While all students whose results appear in the table qualified for Title I services at the beginning of each school year by scoring below the 50th percentile, many of them no longer qualified for Title I services by the end of the year. Beyond the general trend toward improvement in scores, fluctuations in scores within individual classes reflect the natural variations that occur year by year in student populations. Main Street School stopped giving the California Achievement Test after the spring of 2005.

While improvement in students' writing scores were predicted inadvance due to past research data, gains in reading comprehension were not anticipated. After only two years of school-wide implementation, Title I students and Special Education students taking the Gates MacGinitie Reading Comprehensive Test actually outscored the national average of their regular education peers across the country, as shown in Figure A.13.

Table A.1.   California Achievement Test: Title I Grade 2 Total Language Arts Scores

	Percentage of Students in Each Normal Curve Equivalent Range		
	High 99–68	Above Average 67–50	Below Average 49–1
1999	28	50	22
2000	26	53	21
2001	37	26	37
2002	34	53	13
2003	64	36	0
2004	45	45	10
2005	33	61	6

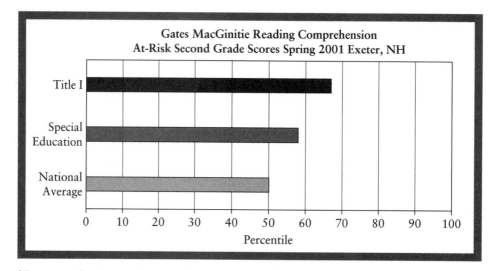

Figure A.13.   Gates MacGinitie Reading Comprehension scores

The Gates MacGinitie Reading Comprehension scores before, during, and after the grant period, document an overall increase in high scores and an overall decrease in low scores of all second-grade students with natural fluctuations occurring due to differences in student populations year to year (see Table A.2).

Table A.2.   Gates MacGinitie: All Grade Two Students

	Percentage of Students in Each Normal Curve Equivalent Range		
	High 99–65	Above Average 64–50	Below Average 49–1
1999 (before schoolwide adoption)	42	36	22
2000	45	38	17
2001	60	30	10
2002	56	34	10
2003	57	27	16
2004	60	28	12
2005	63	30	7
2006	60	23	17
2007	66	22	12

Table A.3. Gates MacGinitie Reading Comprehension Title I, Grade 2; Spring Scores

	Percentage of Title I Students in Each Normal Curve Equivalent Range		
	High 99–65	Above Average 64–50	Below Average 49–1
1999 (before schoolwide adoption)	12	32	56
2002	44	38	18
2003	49	36	15
2004	43	36	21
2005	26	74	0
2006	35	43	23
2007	52	39	9

Looking at the disaggregated Gates MacGinitie data shown in Table A.3, Title I students demonstrated steady improvement, with an increase in high scores and a decrease in low scores. Scores from 2006 in both Table A.2 and Table A.3 reflect a particularly high-need second grade population.

The New Hampshire Educational Improvement and Assessment Program (NHEIAP) was New Hampshire's statewide assessment for many years. State averages were collated for specific subgroups, including many of the groups that are now targeted under No Child Left Behind. Exeter's Title I population has scored significantly higher than the state average for Title I students since 2000, the first full year of the CSRD grant. (See Figure A.14.)

Special Education students have also shown growth on the NHEIAP when compared to the state average for Special Education students. In 2004, 58 percent of the Special Education population scored Basic and above (with possible scores being Novice, Basic, Proficient, and Advanced) when compared to 32 percent for the state average (see Figure A.15).

In 2002, the NHEIAP began reporting scores for socioeconomically disadvantaged students. Exeter's socioeconomically disadvantaged students also scored favorably when compared to the state average for socioeconomically disadvantaged students (O'Connor, 2007). (see Figure A.16.)

The NHEIAP also included a separate Writing Assessment from 1994 to 2003. The results are shown in Figure A.17. Third-grade

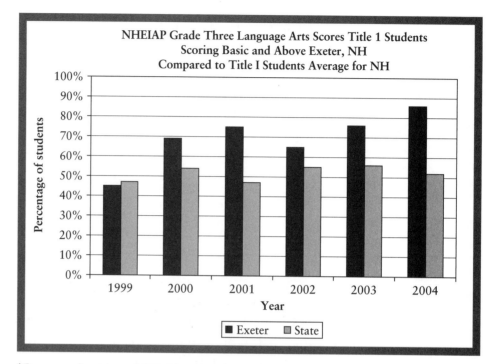

Figure A.14.   NHEIAP Grade 3 Title I scores

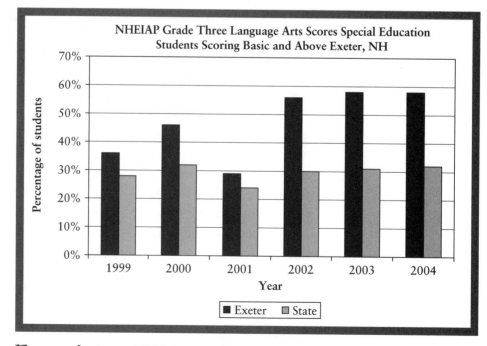

Figure A.15.   NHEIAP Grade 3 Special Education scores

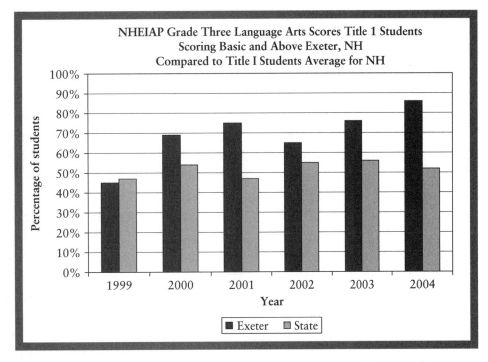

Figure A.16.   NHEIAP Grade 3 Economically Disadvantaged scores

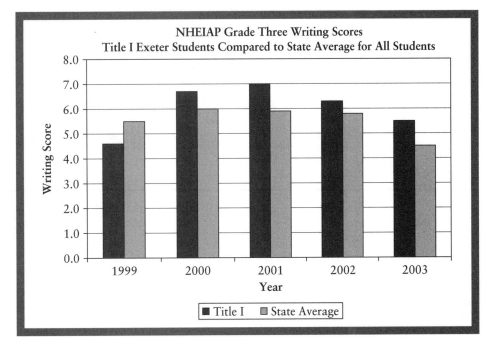

Figure A.17.   NHEIAP Grade 3 Title I Writing scores

students responded to a prompt (usually an essay) in one sitting. One of the most significant findings with the NHEIAP was that, on the Writing Assessment, Exeter's Title I students scored above the state average for all students from 2000 to 2003.

When comparing the NHEIAP standardized test scores of Exeter's students to students across New Hampshire, disaggregated data reveal that Exeter's students have consistently scored better than the state average across all subgroups, with the greatest gains being made by those students within various subgroups exposed to the treatment over time (see Table A.4).

In October 2005, Exeter students took the New England Common Assessment Program (NECAP) for the first time. This statewide assessment was developed to meet the mandates of the No Child Left Behind legislation. The third-grade reading assessment included nine open-response items. Exeter's third-grade Title I, Special Education, and Economically Disadvantaged students all continued to score above the New Hampshire state average for their subgroup (O'Connor, 2007).

Figures A.18 and A.19 document the results of using Picturing Writing in a third-grade classroom in Fowler, California, where 50 percent of the students were English-language learners and 75 percent participated in the Free & Reduced Lunch program. When taking the Siveroli Reading Comprehension Test at the beginning of the school year, 36 percent of the students scored between one and four years

Table A.4.   NHEIAP Grade 3 Language Arts Scores: Disaggregated Data

| Year | Percentage of Students Scoring Basic and Above (state results in parenthesis) | | | |
	All Students	Educational Disability	Title I	Socioeconomically Disadvantaged
1999	79 (72)	36 (28)	45 (47)	not reported
2000	84 (75)	46 (32)	69 (54)	not reported
2001	85 (72)	29 (24)	75 (47)	not reported
2002	84 (76)	56 (30)	65 (55)	56 (55)
2003	89 (76)	58 (31)	76 (56)	67 (58)
2004	88 (73)	58 (32)	86 (52)	86 (54)

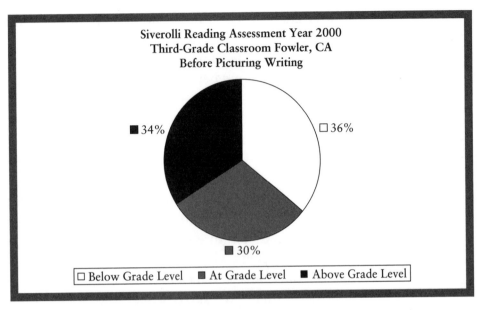

Figure A.18.   Siverolli Reading scores before Picturing Writing

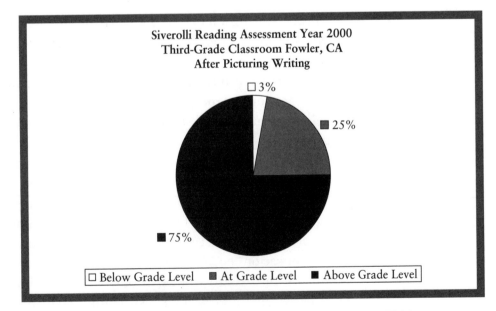

Figure A.19.   Siverolli Reading scores after Picturing Writing

below grade level. After eight months of consistent use of Picturing Writing three times a week, only 3 percent of the students scored below grade level on the same standardized reading test—with 75 percent of the students scoring between three and four years *above* grade level.

Implications

This compilation of quantitative data gathered over sixteen years provides a substantial body of evidence documenting the value of an alternative art-and-literature-based approach to literacy learning, particularly for those students who have already proven time and again that words are not their preferred medium.

Given that "at-risk students" (those who do not perform well on standardized tests—or any tests, for that matter) are currently being targeted under the No Child Left Behind Act, and that traditional straight verbal methods of reading and writing instruction have already proven ineffective for this population, these findings suggest that educators and administrators must broaden the scope of what they consider valid literacy instructional practices if we are to meet the learning needs of *all students* and more effectively address the federal mandate of No Child Left Behind.

These research findings also raise some important questions. While this data documents the powerful role that art can play in improving the literacy learning of all students, it calls into question the validity and effectiveness of our current system for delivering services to those considered to be "at risk." Given the fact that Title I and Special Education students outscored the national and state averages of the regular education students on standardized reading and writing assessments after participating in art-based literacy practices over time, and that Title I and Special Education students consistently outscored their Title I and Special Education peers across the state in statewide language arts assessments, one has to wonder if our narrow, verbocentric methods of delivering reading and writing instruction are in themselves creating a problem. When "low-performing students" consistently outperform their peers (both regular education and those identified as requiring special services) while participating in alternative art-based literacy practices, it is time to take notice. Educators, administrators, and policymakers need to consider whether our educational system is, in fact, creating a class of discouraged, low-achieving students by its very design—and if so, how we might remedy this situation.

The evidence presented in this appendix suggests that adoption of an Artists/Writers Workshop model with its systematic progression of strategically designed and scaffolded art-and-literature-based mini-lessons offers teachers a proven method for improving the literacy learning of all students, particularly those at risk. These findings provide a critical key in resolving what remains a pressing national educational crisis.

Appendix B
Instructional Tools

Facilitators of Artists/Writers Workshops will benefit from a variety of tools and support structures as they help students acquire mental tools for developing, expressing, and recording their ideas in pictures and in words. Although I discuss some of these tools and supporting structures in other chapters in the context of their use, this appendix presents the entire set:

+ Artists Frame
+ Artists/Writers Chair
+ Desktop Easel Stands
+ Word Banks
+ Brainstorming Sheets
+ Accordion Folders
+ Checklists

Most of these items are easy to make from materials readily available in the classroom. (The easel stands are an exception; they must be purchased. The Materials section of the Picturing Writing Web site, www.picturingwriting.org/materials.html, offers reasonably priced desktop easel stands.) If you'd rather avoid the do-it-yourself approach, Artists Frames can be ordered from the Web site as well, along with the recommended watercolors, brushes, paper, and other art supplies that I've found to work well for the art-based writing processes described in this book.

The Artists Frame

The Artists Frame is a simple device used to display works of art during the Group Share. It serves to literally frame and enhance the artwork of the student who is sharing. You can see the Artists Frame being used in the DVD during the two Group Shares that appear in the Artists/ Writers Workshop Overview.

An Artists Frame can be made easily by centering and gluing a piece of black construction paper to a larger piece of white poster board. If student work is on standard letter-size (8.5"×11") paper, I suggest that the black construction paper be at least 9.5"×12" in size so that a black border at least half an inch wide frames the artwork. The poster board should be roughly six to eight inches larger so that the white poster board frames the black construction paper by three or four inches on each side.

If you choose to use the standard seven-inch-square paper mentioned in several of the mini-lessons in Chapter Nine, then the black construction paper needs to be eight inches square and the white poster board closer to fourteen to sixteen inches square (again so you have a white border of poster board roughly three or four inches wide around the black box).

No matter the size, dab the four corners of the black construction paper with a dry glue stick and affix it to the poster board so that it is centered. Then run the poster board through a laminator. (Since paintings are often wet or at least damp during the Group Share, it is helpful to make an Artists Frame that has a surface that can be sponged clean from time to time.) If you don't have access to a laminator, cover the Artists Frame with clear contact paper.

Alternatively, rather than gluing a black construction paper box or rectangle to the poster board, you can stick black electrical tape to the white poster board along the edge of an imagined piece of artwork (depending on the standard size paper you plan on using). This frame should also be laminated or covered with clear contact paper.

Whichever method you choose to construct your Artists Frame, the idea is that when you center a student's artwork in it, a black border (approximately half an inch wide) will show around the student's work. Use a sticky-tack substance or clear mounting squares to temporarily fasten students' artwork onto the Artists Frame.

Artists/Writers Chair

The Artists/Writers Chair evolved out of the idea of the author's chair used in writing workshops (Graves, 1994) and the artist's chair used during artist workshops (Ernst, 1994). It is the designated seat of honor for the student sharing art, or art and writing together. (Remember that when facilitating the art-based writing workshops described in this book, the class would not have occasion to share writing on its own, as students always write to their pictures.)

The Artists/Writers Chair is positioned directly opposite the Artists Frame and is typically placed at the back of the circle or group of students seated on the floor. As Karen Ernst (1994) reminds us, unlike an author's chair, which is positioned at the front of the circle, the Artists Chair should be positioned opposite the frame so that those who are sharing have a good view of their own work during the share process.

If available, a special chair (whether it is painted, stuffed, or is some other way different from the typical student furniture) can enhance the experience of sharing, especially for younger students.

Desktop Easel Stands

Desktop easel stands are used to prop up student artwork during the brainstorming, writing, or revision process. They make it easier for students to see details in their pictures, thus enhancing students' ability read their pictures for detail and description. (Desktop easels can be seen in the DVD during the Artists/Writers Workshop Overview during the Work Session of the Writing Strand).

The stands serve three purposes:

✦ Honor the student's work.
✦ Provide a strong visual focus, particularly helpful to those easily distracted.
✦ Compensate for a possible lack of planar transfer.

"Planar transfer" may be an unfamiliar term. It refers to the ability of the brain to transfer the plane of an image from one plane to another—in this case from horizontal (lying flat on a desk or table) to vertical as it is intended to be viewed. Here is a vivid example shared by my friend and colleague Ann Jule:

Jonathan, a fourth grader who struggled with writing, became very engaged in constructing a collage for the story he was working on. Ann had taped his work-in-progress to the blackboard to make it easier for him to see his evolving image. He worked standing up instead of at his desk, which also suited Jonathan's need to be moving.

As part of his story, Jonathan carefully crafted a picture of a forest that contained several thick, brown, textured tree trunks topped with bright green foliage. Once he completed his collage, he proudly announced to anyone within earshot, "Look, I'm all done. . . . Come look at my picture!"

Then Jonathan proceeded to take his finished collage off the blackboard and place it on his desk. His face immediately went pale. "Oh, no," he wailed. "What's wrong?" asked a classmate. "Look!" Jonathan pointed. "Someone cut down all the trees in my forest! Now my story is ruined!" With his collage flat on the desk, Jonathan saw all his trees as lying on the ground. He was devastated.

Ann—an occupational therapist with a particular interest in neurological development—observed this incident and explained to Jonathan's teacher that it offered a key insight into his brain development. He had not yet developed *planar transfer,* the ability to mentally transfer an image from one plane to another. In other words, his mind did not automatically read the picture that was flat on his desk (on the horizontal plane) as a vertical image (as if the trees were standing upright). Most people take this ability for granted, but it is actually one that is acquired and not by all students at the same time. Lack of planar transfer could be an issue for young students or those with any number of learning difficulties. Easel stands ensure that students view their artwork parallel to their line of vision.

Even those who are able to transfer a horizontal image to the vertical plane find easel stands helpful. Whether or not students are able to articulate why, once you introduce desktop easel stands into your classroom, you will find that everyone is eager to use them. I have had sixth-grade boys (who tower over me in height) ask if they may borrow an easel stand overnight while they work on revising their writing. Students of all ages seem to understand that the desktop easels support their writing process along with their art.

Third-grade Grayson says it best: "I learned that after you paint your pictures it is much easier to write because you have all the details you need right in front of you. And when you have like a stand to hold it up, it is much easier to see it."

Easel stands can also be used to prop up books when students are engaged in visual research such as sketching or creating fact-based art.

Word Banks

Word banks provide students with theme-based palettes of colorful language with which to paint pictures, as described in Chapter Five. Capture the silver dollar words the class brainstorms in theme-related lists and post them on the walls as word banks. You can also type them up and place them in students' writing folders or in student thesauruses to make these words available to those students who may not retain them simply through discussion.

Once students understand that they have lots of options as they begin to craft their language, they often find themselves going to the word banks to select the very best words to use to paint a picture of what is happening in their picture.

Brainstorming Sheets

The brainstorming process expands word choice, and it also forces transmediation to occur by asking students to look at the important things in a picture and attach verbal language to them. If students do not have the

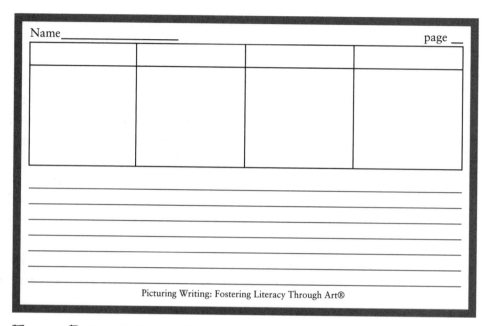

Figure B.1.   Brainstorming sheet.

opportunity to orally rehearse their work, it is during the brainstorming process that they begin to translate a visual thought into words. In either case, with or without oral rehearsal, having to look at their picture, identify the important things, and brainstorm silver dollar words opens up the world of crafting language, which may otherwise be overlooked.

As discussed in Chapter Five, the most basic brainstorming sheet is a simple four-column open-ended form designed to activate deep looking and reading of each picture, combined with a set of lines for writing. Figure 5.2 shows a sample of a completed brainstorming sheet, and Figure B.1 shows a brainstorming sheet that has not been used.

Use of the brainstorming sheet is described in Chapters Five and Nine and modeled in the Artists/Writers Workshop Overview on the DVD.

Accordion Folders

The "accordion folder," an easy-to-make organizational tool developed by first-grade teacher Joyce Bosch, provides a convenient way for students to keep their work in proper sequence. This handy tool—constructed out of sheets of oak tag (or tag board) taped together—has grown far beyond its original purpose as a sequencing tool. For teachers, it provides an overarching organizational structure for designing and delivering literature-based mini-lessons and modeling sessions. For students, the accordion folder makes sequencing the literary elements and subtopics in report-writing concrete.

With each panel of the accordion folder, labeled according to the shared purpose of pictures and words for that page, students come to understand that each panel, and thus each picture and page of writing to be created and paper-clipped to that panel, has its own specific purpose. Supported by teacher-facilitated literature-based mini-lessons and modeling sessions, students create art and writing to address the identified purpose of each panel of the accordion folder. Each completed picture and each page of writing is then paper-clipped to the appropriate panel.

While the accordion folder allows students to enter the art and writing process with purpose, it also embodies the underlying premise of Artists/Writers Workshop: that the language of pictures and the language of words can serve a common purpose. The accordion folder offers the concrete embodiment of the parallel and complementary nature of pictures and words.

Multiple Uses

The accordion folder can be designed to support creating a simple time of day sequence, a story sequence (with each panel labeled with a literary element such as setting, character, problem, solution, and ending), or a report. In the last case, each panel of the accordion folder can be labeled with a subtopic. For instance, a report on an endangered animal might contain panels labeled Habitat; Physical Characteristics; Food or Prey; Predators; Interesting Facts; Why Endangered. Or the study of the life cycle of the monarch butterfly may use the panels of the accordion folder to identify and organize research information gathered around each stage of the cycle. When a research report is approached in this manner, students create one picture to address each subtopic or each panel of the accordion folder and once again write to that picture, drawing on the facts they have gathered on that topic. (Keep in mind that creating pictures using visual resources can be a form of research in itself.)

Making an Accordion Folder

The accordion folder is a simple device created out of several sheets of 9"×12" oak tag that are taped together using masking tape to create an accordion. (Alternatively, you can fold 12"×18" oak tag to create two panels and tape those sheets together.)

Construction is easy. Line up several sheets of oak tag either vertically or horizontally, depending on the size and shape of the artwork your students will be creating. (To accommodate horizontal artwork, oak tag should be taped along the 9" end of the sheet to create a horizontal accordion. To accommodate vertical or square artwork, oak tag panels should be taped along the 12" edge to create a vertical folder. Use three sheets of oak tag for a three-panel story, and five for a five-panel story. Fasten the panels together fanwise, with masking tape along their common edges. With a black marker, label the inside panels of the accordion folder as desired at the bottom center. Some teachers prefer to write directly on the oak tag while others create handwritten or typed sticky labels. Label the outside front panel "Cover" and the outside back panel "About the Artist/Writer."

As students create pictures and text, they paperclip their art and writing onto the appropriate panel of their accordion folder. If possible, hand out large plastic paperclips for this purpose to avoid rust marks, indentations, or scratches that metal paperclips can leave on student artwork. Large paperclips are also easier for students to handle and do a better job of fastening.

Accordion folders are generally stored inside a pocket folder, thus providing protection for the folder as well as handy pockets for loose pieces of paper such as sketches, research, storyboards, word banks, and checklists.

Checklists

A variety of checklists can be designed to meet the needs of students at various grade levels. Checklists can range from task-oriented lists to help students (and teachers) keep track of students' progress as they move through the art and writing process to reminders about the inclusion of certain elements for each picture or page of writing on each panel of the accordion folder. Checklists can also be used to address editing and revision as well. Checklists developed as reminders during the process can be used as assessment tools later on.

References

Cited References

Anderson, R. C., Hiebert, E. H., Scott, J. A., & Wilkinson, I. A. G. (1985). *Becoming a Nation of Readers*. Washington, DC: National Institute of Education.

Bandura, A. (1997). *Self-Efficacy: The Exercise of Control*. New York: Freeman.

Bell, N. (1991). *Visualizing and Verbalizing for Language Comprehension and Thinking*. San Luis Obispo, CA: Gander.

Berghoff, B., Borgmann, C. B., & Parr, C. (2003). "Cycles of Inquiry With the Arts." *Language Arts, 80*(45), 353–362.

Brudnak, K. (1995). "Reach Every Student." *Learning Magazine, 23*(4), 53–56.

Caine, G., & Caine, R. N. (1994). *Making Connections: Teaching and the Human Brain*. Menlo Park, CA: Addison-Wesley.

Cowan, K., & Albers, P. (2006). "Semiotic Representations: Building Complex Literacy Practices Through the Arts." *The Reading Teacher, 60*(2), 124–137.

Deasey, R. J., ed. (2002). *Critical Links: Learning in the Arts and Student Academic and Social Development*. Washington, DC: Arts Education Partnership.

Eisner, E. W. (1998). "Does Experience in the Arts Boost Academic Achievement?" *Art Education, 51*(1), 7–15.

Ernst, K. (1994). *Picturing Learning*. Portsmouth, NH: Heinemann.

Fletcher, R., & Portalupi, J. (1998). *Craft Lessons*. York, ME: Stenhouse.

Freed, J., & Parsons, L. (1997). *Right-Brained Children in a Left-Brained World*. New York: Simon & Schuster.

Gardner, H. (1983). *Frames of Mind: The Theory of Multiple Intelligences*. New York: Basic Books.

Given, B. K. (2008). Personal Communication.

Graves, D. (1994). *A Fresh Look at Writing*. Portsmouth, NH: Heinemann.

Howard, M. A. D., & Anderson, R. J. (1978). "Early Identification of Potential School Dropouts." *Child Welfare, 52,* 221–31.

Kelly, F. J., Veldman, D. J., & McGuire, C. (1964). "Multiple Discriminant Prediction of Delinquency and School Dropouts." *Educational and Psychological Measurement 24.*

Lloyd, D. N. (1978). "Prediction of School Failure from Third Grade Data." *Educational and Psychological Measurement 38.*

Marcus, L. S. (2002). *Ways of Telling: Conversations on the Art of the Picture Book.* New York: Dutton Children's Books.

McClanahan, R. (1999). *Word Painting: A Guide to Writing More Descriptively.* Cincinnati, OH: Writer's Digest Books.

McPartland, J. M., & Slavin, R. E. (1990). *Policy Perspectives: Increasing Achievement of At-Risk Students at Each Grade Level.* Washington, DC: Office of Educational Research and Improvement, U.S. Department of Education.

O'Connor, S. (2007). "Picturing Writing/Image-Making standardized test score data," Exeter, NH. Presented at the 2007 NCTE Convention in New York on November 15, 2007.

Olshansky, B. (1992). *Children as Authors, Children as Illustrators: The Whole Story* (videotape). Portsmouth, NH: Heinemann.

Olshansky, B. (1998). *Image-Making Within The Writing Process: Crafting Collage Stories.* Durham, NH: Center for the Advancement of Art-Based Literacy, University of New Hampshire.

Olson, J. L. (1992). *Envisioning Writing.* Portsmouth, NH: Heinemann.

Routman, R. (1997). *Invitations: Changing as Teachers and Learners, K–12.* Portsmouth, NH: Heinemann.

Siegel, M. (1995). "More than words: The Generative Power of Transmediation for Learning." *Canadian Journal of Education/Revue canadienne de l'éducation, 20*(4), 455–475.

Sperry, R. (1968). "Hemisphere Disconnection and Unity in Conscious Awareness."*American Psychologist, 23,* 723–733.

Vygotsky, L. S. (1978). *Mind in Society: Development of Higher Psychological Processes.* Cambridge, MA: Harvard University Press.

West, T. G. (1991). *In the Mind's Eye.* Buffalo, NY: Prometheus Books.

Winner, E. & Cooper, M. (2000). "Mute Those Claims: No Evidence (Yet) for a Causal Link Between Arts Study and Academic Achievement." *Journal of Aesthetic Education, 34*(3–4), 11–75.

Wood Ray, K. (2004). When Kids Make Books. *Educational Leadership, 62*(2), 15.

Wood Ray, K. & Cleaveland, L. (2004). *About the Authors.* Portsmouth, NH: Heinemann.

Children's Books

Berger, B. (1984). *Grandfather Twilight*. New York: Putnam.

Brautigam, N. (1995). *The Best Winter of All*. Durham, NH: Laboratory for Interactive Learning, University of New Hampshire.

Carle, E. (1993). *Eric Carle: Picture Writer* (video), New York: Philomel Books.

Clark, A. (1995). *Sarena and the Beautiful Skies*. Durham, NH: Laboratory for Interactive Learning, University of New Hampshire.

Chase, E. N. (1996). *Secret Dawn*. Buffalo, NY: Firefly Books.

Collins, P. L. (1992). *I Am An Artist*. Brookfield, CT: Millbrook Press.

Cragnoline, J. (1995). *Someone Special*. Durham, NH: Laboratory for Interactive Learning, University of New Hampshire.

DePaola, T. (1988). *The Legend of the Indian Paintbrush*. New York: Putnam.

Fletcher, R. (1997). *Twilight Comes Twice*. New York: Clarion Books.

Hall, D. (1979). *Oxcart Man*. New York: Puffin Books.

Honda, T. (1992). *Wild Horse Winter*. San Francisco: Chronicle Books.

Gibbons, G. (1994). *Wolves*. New York: Holiday House.

Larsen, K. (1998). *Sunset Dream*. Durham, NH: Laboratory for Interactive Learning, University of New Hampshire.

Lewis, R. (1965). *In a Spring Garden*. New York: Dial Books for Young Readers.

Locker, T. (1997). *Water Dance*. New York: Harcourt Brace.

Locker, T. (2001). *Mountain Dance*. New York: Harcourt Brace.

Locker, T., & Bruchac, J. (2004). *Rachel Carson: Preserving a Sense of Wonder*. Golden, CO: Fulcrum.

Luenn, N. (1992). *Mother Earth*. New York: Aladdin Books.

Marzollo, J. (1995). *Sun Song*. New York: HarperCollins.

Olshansky, B. (2000). *The Sun's Day*. Durham, NH: Center for the Advancement of Art-Based Literacy, University of New Hampshire.

Wood, A. (1997). *Quick As a Cricket*. Wiltshire, England: Child's Play.

Yolen, J. (1987). *Owl Moon*. New York: Philomel Books.

Index

Contents of the DVD

Artists/Writers Workshop

Chapter One: Artists/Writers Workshop Overview (28 minutes)

- ✦ Introduction
- ✦ Art Strand
  - • Literature Share
  - • Modeling Session
  - • Work Session
  - • Group Share
- ✦ Writing Strand
  - • Literature Share
  - • Modeling Session
  - • Work Session
  - • Group Share
- ✦ Student Reflections

Chapter Two: Introduction to Watercolor on Wet Paper (3 minutes)

Chapter Three: Introduction to Crayon Resist (7 minutes)